MESSAGE OF THE FATHERS OF THE CHURCH

General Editor: Thomas Halton

Volume 14

MESSAGE OF THE FATHERS OF THE CHURCH

TEACHING AUTHORITY IN THE EARLY CHURCH

by

Robert B. Eno, S.S.

Michael Glazier, Inc.
Wilmington, Delaware

ABOUT THE AUTHOR

Robert B. Eno, S.S., holds his doctorate in theology from Institute Catholique de Paris. His work in ecumenical and historical studies is widely recognized, and he has devoted much research to the focal question of doctrinal authority. He is on the faculty of the Catholic University of America.

First published in 1984 by Michael Glazier, Inc.,
1723 Delaware Avenue, Wilmington, Delaware 19806

©1984 by Michael Glazier, Inc. All rights reserved

Library of Congress Catalog Card Number: 83-83253
International Standard Book Number:
   Message of the Fathers of the Church series:
      (0-89453-312-6, Paper; 0-89453-340-1, Cloth)
      TEACHING AUTHORITY IN THE EARLY CHURCH
      (0-89453-325-8, Paper)
      (0-89453-354-1, Cloth)

Cover design by Lillian Brulc

Typography by Richard Reinsmith

Printed in the United States of America

CONTENTS

5

Chapter Four
Other Third Century Developments

Chapter Five
Conflicts and Tradition: The Church of the Empire

Abbreviations

CCL	*Corpus Christianorum, Series Latina*
CSEL	*Corpus Scriptorum Ecclesiasticorum Latinorum*
GCS	*Die griechischen christlichen Schriftsteller der ersten drei Jahrhunderte*
PG	*Patrologia Graeca*
PL	*Patrologia Latina*
SC	*Sources Chrétiennes*

EDITOR'S INTRODUCTION

The *Message of the Fathers of the Church* is a companion series to *The Old Testament Message* and *The New Testament Message*. It was conceived and planned in the belief that Scripture and Tradition worked hand in hand in the formation of the thought, life and worship of the primitive Church. Such a series, it was felt, would be a most effective way of opening up what has become virtually a closed book to present-day readers, and might serve to stimulate a revival in interest in Patristic studies in step with the recent, gratifying resurgence in Scriptural studies.

The term "Fathers" is usually reserved for Christian writers marked by orthodoxy of doctrine, holiness of life, ecclesiastical approval and antiquity. "Antiquity" is generally understood to include writers down to Gregory the Great (+604) or Isidore of Seville (+636) in the West, and John Damascene (+749) in the East. In the present series, however, greater elasticity has been encouraged, and quotations from writers not noted for orthodoxy will sometimes be included in order to illustrate the evolution of the Message on particular doctrinal matters. Likewise, writers later than the mid-eighth century will sometimes be used to illustrate the continuity of tradition on matters like sacramental theology or liturgical practice.

An earnest attempt was made to select collaborators on a broad inter-disciplinary and inter-confessional basis, the chief consideration being to match scholars who could handle the Fathers in their original languages with subjects in which they had already demonstrated a special interest and competence. About the only editorial directive given to the selected contributors was that the Fathers, for the most part, should be allowed to speak for themselves and that they should speak in readable, reliable modern English. Volumes on individual themes were considered more suitable than volumes devoted to individual Fathers, each theme, hopefully, contributing an important segment to the total mosaic of the Early Church, one, holy, catholic and apostolic. Each volume has an introductory essay outlining the historical and theological development of the theme, with the body of the work mainly occupied with liberal citations from the Fathers in modern English translation and a minimum of linking commentary. Short lists of Suggested Further Readings are included; but dense, scholarly footnotes were actively discouraged on the pragmatic grounds that such scholarly shorthand has other outlets and tends to lose all but the most relentlessly esoteric reader in a semi-popular series.

At the outset of his *Against Heresies* Irenaeus of Lyons warns his readers "not to expect from me any display of rhetoric, which I have never learned, or any excellence of composition, which I have never practised, or any beauty or persuasiveness of style, to which I make no pretensions." Similarly, modest disclaimers can be found in many of the Greek and Latin Fathers and all too often, unfortunately, they have been taken at their word by an uninterested world. In fact, however, they were often highly educated products of the best rhetorical schools of their day in the Roman Empire, and what they have to say is often as much a lesson in literary and cultural, as well as in spiritual, edification.

St. Augustine, in *The City of God* (19.7), has interesting reflections on the need for a common language in an expanding world community; without a common language a man is more at home with his dog than with a foreigner as far as intercommunication goes, even in the Roman Empire, which imposes on the nations it conquers the yoke of both law and language with a resultant abundance of interpreters. It is hoped that in the present world of continuing language barriers the contributors to the series will prove opportune interpreters of the perennial Christian message.

Thomas Halton

INTRODUCTION

The first thing about the religious scene in Europe and North America that might strike the visitor to our planet would be no doubt the multiplicity of Christian confessions and denominations. Upon further enquiry, he would find that each denomination believed that it, unlike the others, or, at least, to a greater degree than the others, was following the teachings of Christ as these were recorded in the New Testament and handed down over the centuries of Christian history. Our spatial visitor would quickly conclude that such claims by so many differing groups could not be sustained.

This book concerns a variety of issues, including tradition, orthodoxy, church office, all revolving around the general question of teaching authority. Ecumenists today usually conclude that behind every difference among Christians lies the question of teaching authority in the Church. Who is authorized to make ultimate decisions about what the faith is? What are we to believe? What are Christians to do in given circumstances, faced with concrete moral dilemmas? The multiplicity of denominations, the variations on the basic themes of Christian faith, some major, some minor, testify to the divergent views on authority among Christians.

Since this is a volume of patristic readings, it must take

for granted some of the ancient presuppositions, although people are aware today that these are in fact less certain than once thought. So we shall not enter into such questions as whether or not Jesus founded a Church or precisely what Jesus' teachings were about any issue. These two questions are obviously basic. The answers were taken for granted by the Fathers: viz., that Jesus intended to found a Church and did so; that he had a certain clear corpus of teachings which he entrusted to his disciples, principally the Twelve or later, the Twelve Apostles. Hence in the patristic era and since, the essential adjective of authority has been "*apostolic.*" Indeed 'apostolic' has become one of the four classic marks of the Church.

A Static View

The Fathers thus manifest what has been called the "classic world view or mentality," one that is largely static, that looks to the past, for which unity is superior to multiplicity, the unchanging to the changing. Preservation of the treasures from the past is the keynote. Generally, there is manifested relatively little consciousness of ideas of development and change. As someone has quipped, the last thing a theologian of the ancient or medieval periods would have wanted to be called was "an original mind." Tradition, in the sense of simply handing on the inheritance of the past, was at a premium. Nothing was to be added to doctrine; nothing subtracted from it.

As we shall see, rare was the Father who adverted to the idea of progress in doctrine. Eusebius of Caesarea believed he was breaking new ground in his *Church History* (I.1.3). Gregory of Nazianzus (*Orat.* 31.27) showed that he was aware that there had earlier been little discussion of the question of the divinity of the Holy Spirit. He speculated briefly and in passing about "new light breaking upon us little by little." Here such Gospel sayings as Jn 14.26 might apply. What could be more appropriate than that one of the things the Spirit would teach the Faithful would be the full truth about Himself? Such speculations, however, were the exception.

For most, the teachings of Christ were simply there. The idea of a clear, compact, unambiguous series of teachings or doctrines coming from Christ held sway. The principal image here was that of the "deposit." One almost had the vision literally of a trunk or large hope-chest into which the Apostles had placed the clear teachings of Christ neatly wrapped as a body of doctrine. Succeeding generations were to keep it safe, stand guard over it, not allowing anything else to be put into it nor anything to be taken out and discarded.

As is the case with any historical study, when we look at documents of the past, there are several things which must be kept in mind. One of the primary questions we must ask is: Why is this being said? What is the problem or error that causes this to be said, this point to be made rather than some other point? In addition to the classical tendency to look to the past, to concentrate on unchanging essences, another possible factor for the early Christian bias in favor of the unchanging was its most threatening early opponent, the general movement we call Gnosticism. This tendency, in its penchant for the esoteric, strange-sounding and exotic names and titles, its inherent appeal to a certain type of intellectual pretension and social sophistication, prided itself upon its unending search for the truth. "Seek and you shall find" was, according to the Fathers, their favorite verse of the New Testament. Like Lessing, they took much greater delight in the search than in any possible finding. With such a powerful opponent fostering flux in understanding, it is not surprising that main-line Christian teachers should have put so much emphasis on stability and solidity in teaching.

Revelation: Deposit of Faith Versus Conflicting Theologies

But the problem of divergencies in Christian teaching, the inability to agree on what it was that Christ taught, is not just something that appears in the second or third century. This apparently has always been the case in the history of Christianity. Some radical critics, such as Walter Bauer, have tried to deny that there ever was something that might accurately be called "orthodoxy." For them, the teaching of Jesus himself remains largely an unknown. There were very many who soon professed to present Jesus' teaching but they contradicted each other. In different parts of the Near East, widely varying versions of Christianity dominated at first. They claim, finally, that one form won out, declared itself orthodox, and condemned all other versions as heretical or heterodox.

While not going this far, many exegetes, including many Catholics, now recognize a variety of theological perspectives in the first Christian century and in the New Testament itself. Thus Ernst Käsemann can say that he sees the New Testament as the basis of the Church's diversity more than of its unity. More often, however, commentators, while admitting diversity in the New Testament do not admit contradictions.

What evidence is there for conflict in the earliest churches? Paul in particular notes the divergences between his view of the Jewish Law and that of more conservative individuals and groups who combat and contradict his teachings. More significantly for our purposes, the three so-called Pastoral epistles to Timothy and Titus, which most critics no longer consider to be authentically Pauline, give evidence of the growing problem for the early Church of doctrinal divergence. Here the keynote is sounded, one that will be foundational for the future: "*O Timothy, guard what has been committed to you.* (The deposit: Parathēkē). *Stay clear of worldly, idle talk and the contradictions of what is falsely called knowledge* (Gnosis) " (1 Tm 6.20). The Pastoral epistles show not only the concern over divergent teachings and traditions within the New Testament itself, but also that one form of solution, or at least one attempted defense, is coming to the fore: the growing authority invested in the leaders of the Church, specifically in those who hold office in the local church, those who in one way or another are looked upon as inheriting the apostolic mantle.

This attitude toward the past, the view of Christ's teaching as a deposit committed to an authoritative group of leaders ("The Twelve"; "The Apostles") in turn will inevitably bring about a corollary: (using the terms of later theology) the view that revelation ended with the death of the last Apostle. Whatever its precise theology of revelation, later generations of believers have always looked back to the time of the "Fathers," more precisely to the time of the New Testament, the first Christian century, the time of Jesus and the Apostles, as a very special period, a period that is constitutive for the rest of the Church in a way that other periods are not and can never be. This view can be exaggerated insofar as it may look at the first century as something that is totally different from all other periods, a time exempt from the troubles and shortcomings of later centuries, a period somehow not subject to historical criticism.

Trustees of the Deposit

Divergent views of the nature of revelation are basic to one's view of doctrinal authority. If revelation is a deposit left behind at the end of the first and beginning of the second Christian centuries, to be guarded, then it is less surprising to see that a select group of Church officer-leaders come to be considered the trustees of this deposit. These are the ones who teach what is in the deposit and only that. They are to fight off attempts to change or distort the deposit. Hence the "classic" theory of heresy as enunciated by Tertullian — the truth comes first and imitations/counterfeits come later. This presupposes that all elements of the faith were not only present but were clearly explicit from the very beginning. As we know, this is, to say the least, an over-simplified view.

Preserving intact the deposit is one thing but even this preservative task cannot be fulfilled without making explicit what was only implicit previously. Questions not asked before, nor even thought of, must now be faced and answers found, answers compatible with what has been explicitly known. The real problem for these guardians of the original deposit begins when new questions have to be answered and new perspectives integrated. Hence in fact, whether they realized it or not, the patristic viewpoint was not as static as its own theory demanded simply because it could not have remained so and survived.

To take one example: the principal explicitly theological questions for the early Church were trinitarian and christological questions. Christians prided themselves on being monotheists over against the many gods and idols of the pagans, whose worship they, like the Jews, never ceased to mock. Yet in Christian tradition and especially in the prayer, devotional and liturgical life of Christians, Christ was honored as divine. Were there two gods or one? Were Christians monotheists or not? A variety of unacceptable solutions were floated, unacceptable because they did not satisfactorily explain the belief that Christ was fully divine. Thus the so-called classic theory — that all of Christian doctrine was clear and explicit from the beginning, that the Apostles knew all of it, cannot be sustained historically. Indeed, as has been frequently pointed out, those teachings ultimately rejected as heretical or unacceptable at least performed the service of forcing Christians to think about questions that had previously been vague and unexplored.

The Montanist Threat

The idea of a closed revelation has all sorts of implications. Yet there have been other possibilities. The possibility of a literally ongoing revelation is one of the most radical of these. In this context, the Montanist movement of the second century comes to mind. This movement arose in Asia Minor, particularly in the province of Phrygia. Here Montanus, a former pagan priest, began to prophesy. He claimed that the Paraclete spoke directly through him and his two female prophetesses, Priscilla and Maximilla. Initially at least, Montanism as its adversaries called it, did not seem to advocate heresies in the strict sense. Rather it represented a call for a stricter discipline and for the revival of the charism of prophecy in the Church. Hence they referred to themselves as "the New Prophecy." However, judging from the type of personal invective and probably just plain slander one finds thrown against them in Eusebius' *Church History*, Montanism was regarded as a notable threat, not because of its call for a stricter way of life but because, in principle, the notion of the Spirit speaking in an ongoing way through prophets went against the developing consensus of the idea of a closed revelation, a clear-cut deposit whose guardianship and interpretation were entrusted to the leaders of the institutional Church.

As the history of the Church unfolded, there would be other types of non-hierarchical authority in the Church. First, there were the martyrs and confessors from the time of persecution. Here, as in the case of Cyprian of Carthage in the mid-third century, there was conflict over a disciplinary question: What to do about sinners, the lapsed Christians? Later the successors of the martyrs, the monks and holy men (who generally were not clerics) could sometimes threaten to develop into rivals of the clergy and hierarchy. Their existence and witness brought to the fore a perennial problem — the contrast between the moral authority of men and women who seem to lead the Christian life in a fuller and more committed way versus the institutional and doctrinal authority of men who, as Christians, may well seem less impressive, if not positively scandalous. This problem was at least partially overcome by the growing practice of making monks bishops.

The Magisterium of the Bishops

But despite challenges, the basic role of authority in the Church in matters of doctrine early devolved upon, and remained with, the leaders of the local churches, the bishops. And, despite some variations, the presumption of the deposit idea of a revelation given once for all has continued to dominate. The theology of the magisterium, made explicit in modern times, goes back to this idea. It is interesting to compare it to the role of the constitution and the ongoing interpretation of the Supreme Court in the United States. The Founding Fathers of the United States of America could not have foreseen all the developments that have taken place in the world over the past two centuries. Some authoritative body has to exist to make decisions about ongoing laws and legal decisions in relation to the original Constitution. Has the Supreme Court, strict constructionist or not, interpreted the laws in accordance with the Constitution or in violation of it? Is it simply useless to pose the question in such terms? Has the Court in effect changed the Constitution? And if so, was this not inevitable? In some way, the modern Roman Catholic notion of the Magisterium of Pope and bishops raises analogous questions. How did this development begin? What were the authorities for the early Church and how were they connected with later developments in Church history?

The Authority of Holy Scripture

In studying the Fathers, one is struck by the omnipresence of Scripture. The Fathers' works are homilies on Scripture, commentaries on Scripture. In their other works, be they polemical against Jews or heretics, or works discussing some point of doctrine, Scripture is cited page after page. For the Fathers, the teaching of Christ as passed on by the Apostles is the supreme authority. The word "apostolic" is invoked repeatedly. The teaching of Christ and of the Apostles is to be found in Scripture. This, of course, very much includes the Old Testament especially as interpreted "spiritually" (allegorically or figuratively) to show Christ's presence and activity in the Old Covenant. As St. Augustine, writing against the Donatists who put so much emphasis on the opinions of St. Cyprian, put it:

> "Who is unaware that canonical Scripture, the Old as well as the New Testament...is to be put before all later

writings of bishops so that the truth and correctness of whatever one finds there can neither be called into doubt or discussed? On the other hand, all the writings of bishops since the establishment of the canon of Scripture can be criticized by the wiser view of someone who knows more about a question or by the greater authority and prudence of other bishops if it should happen that these writings stray from the truth..."

(*On Baptism* II.3.4)

The difficulty then as now is not the supremacy of Scripture but what that means in practice. All parties to every dispute claim to base their position on Scripture. As Tertullian put it c. 200 A.D., the only practical result from a debate with heretics in which each side parades its scriptural "evidence" is a headache or a stomach ache. He added: "What is the first thing a heretic brings up to try to convince you? 'It is written...'." While the Fathers look to Scripture, they in fact must have other criteria which will be decisive in determining the meaning of Scripture. One of the most important of these is Tradition, the way the Church has (at least with some consistency) interpreted Scripture in the past. It does no good simply to cite Scripture, if the interpretation conflicts with or leads to conflict with the way the Church has usually understood something. So if "Jesus answered: Why do you call me good? No one is good but God alone?" (Mk 10.18), were brought forward as proof of the non-divinity of Christ, such an interpretation would be rejected as incompatible with the totality of Scripture and incompatible with the Church's traditional belief. Or as Tertullian put it: "We do not take our scriptural teaching from the parables but we interpret the parables according to our teaching." (*On Purity*. 9.1; cf. *The Prescription Against the Heretics*. 38.10). Scripture is the basis of teaching — yes, but Scripture is to be interpreted in accordance with the Church's traditional teaching, not contrary to it. If the letter of Scripture seems to contradict that tradition, then one must assume that the passage in question is not being interpreted correctly. An atomistic interpretation of Scripture will inevitably lead to difficulties and misunderstandings. The Scriptures come from God and therefore must be consistent with themselves, having ultimately a single divine author.

The Rule of Faith

Given the disputes over the interpretation of Scripture, one of the key elements in the early Church's understanding of its teaching was the Rule of Faith (*Regula Fidei*; *Regula Veritatis*; *Regula Pietatis*; *Kanōn tēs Pisteōs*). First, the Rule of Faith was a short statement of the Church's belief. It was not some kind of measuring stick or external criterion which could be applied to doctrines to test their acceptability. It is not what much later Catholic theology would call the "analogy of faith." The Rule of Faith is the Faith itself, i.e. the brief statement of articles of belief. It is not precisely the same thing as a creed, though it constitutes one element which contributed to the later development of creeds.

The relationship of the Rule of Faith to early baptismal symbols or declarations of faith made by those to be baptized or by the baptizing minister in interrogatory form as in Hippolytus' *Apostolic Tradition*, is not clear. The later creeds of conciliar origin became increasingly complex because of the need to combat in a more explicit form various errors as they arose. Finally, the general opinion of scholars holds that there was no one fixed text for the Rule of Faith. Basically, the same elements are always found with somewhat different wording or order.

Who Has Apostolic Authority?

Yet this Rule of Faith, however clear and succinct in comparison to Scripture, sooner or later presents the same problem. It needs to be interpreted; in itself it cannot answer all the questions and problems that arise. Here the connection with the Apostles, and through the Apostles to Christ, becomes of special importance. Who in the Church has this special connection? In one sense, the whole Church has this connection because the Church is apostolic. How is this connection established? Who in the Church is able in an authentic way to teach and interpret both the Scriptures and the Rule of Faith?

The Gnostic Threat

First, before seeking an answer, we should see who the principal opponents were at this time. In general, we will call them the Gnostics who laid claim to possession by an elite few of a special esoteric knowledge that explained to people who they were and how they came to be there. This doctrine generally dissociated God the Father, the Creator God, from Jesus whom they saw as the son of the supreme God, the good God. Following upon this, some of them, Marcion notably, maintained that the Hebrew Scripture, coming from the Creator God were to be rejected as totally different from, and inferior to, the teachings of Jesus. Main-line Christians, of course, rejected such ideas, claiming that their teaching came from Jesus through the Apostles. The difficulty was that the Gnostics also claimed apostolic authority for their teaching. They asserted that their teaching was handed down in a secret tradition through a series of teachers going back to a particular apostle who, in turn, received it as a secret teaching from Jesus. Hence the Gnostics ridiculed the Christian Scripture as weak doctrine for spiritual infants, not the real and profound teaching of Jesus which was not meant for the masses. How to answer such a claim?

The Church's argument as developed principally by Irenaeus and Tertullian maintained that the only logical presumption was that Jesus taught his real doctrine to his disciples and that they in turn taught the same in its totality to their followers, especially those whom they set over the local communities. In other words, they opposed a public, historically verifiable tradition of teaching to an alleged, secret, unverifiable tradition. Hence the importance of the appeal to the local churches founded by Apostles. As Tertullian put it, if you wish to find out what the Apostles really taught, you do not go to private, i.e. Gnostic teachers, who claim, but cannot offer proof, that their teachings derive from an authentic tradition. Rather you go to those cities and towns where there are Christian communities founded by Apostles. Moreover, these congregations can also give proof not only of apostolic foundation but of an historically demonstrable link with the apostolic generation. This, of course, was the list of their community leaders, their bishops. These leaders, from the first one appointed by the founding Apostle down to the current president, had as their duty to teach and to hand on only what they had received from Christ through the Apostle. The conclusive proof of the authenticity of this teaching according to Irenaeus and Tertullian, was the unity of the teaching put forward in the Church as a whole. The churches had the same Rule of Faith; among the Gnostic teachers, on the contrary, each had his own version of the secret teaching. The Gnostic teachers, then, differed widely among themselves; indeed, the disciple usually changed some aspect of his master's doctrine to demonstrate his own originality. This was a further proof of the Catholic case. As Tertullian added: Other newly founded churches were also apostolic through a "kinship in teaching" because they also taught the apostolic doctrine they received from the older churches. But it was these older, local churches that were essential to the argument. Even earlier than Irenaeus and Tertullian, the Jewish Christian author, Hegesippus, mentions that he visited some of the apostolically founded churches around the Mediterranean and found they all taught the same doctrine. The continuity of teaching is basically what makes a local church apostolic so long as it teaches what the Apostles taught. Eventually, of course, many churches founded by Apostles historically would be lost to Christendom, largely or wholly in the post-patristic period. It is primarily a question of teaching and only secondarily a question of historical links. The fact of the historical link and the fact of unity of teaching form the practical evidence of continuity.

Within the local church, the person on whom this function of symbolizing the unity of the Church both as link with the other local churches and as center around which local Christians are to rally is the leader of the local community, the bishop. In modern Roman Catholic theology, the idea of succession and continuity have concentrated inordinately on the idea of a succession of validly ordained bishops. The patristic view centered rather on 1) apostolicity of teaching and 2) from the second century, the fact of one bishop in lawful succession to his predecessor in a given see. While the Church or community as a whole was entrusted with the teaching, it was in fact the leader in particular who, embodying the unity of the Church, was also its teacher par excellence.

The Ministry of Teaching

Was it thus from the beginning? In fact, the precise form taken by the ministry of the Church has long been a subject of debate. The founding Apostle of whom we have spoken above, belonged to a unique and unrepeatable ministry; as later bishops were not apostles, so the original Apostles were not bishops. As far as we can tell, the earliest Christian communities had more of a collective than individualistic leadership. What we know of the earliest Jerusalem community from *Acts* and the account in Eusebius' *Church History* seems to show James and his immediate successors as holding a pre-eminent position as individuals even though they were aided by a group of elders/presbyters. In other communities that we know of, especially among gentile Christians, the collectivity of leadership was more pronounced. Leaders were variously designated *episkopoi* or *presbyteroi* but the distinction between the groups was usually blurred. Were there several *episkopoi* in the community? Were some of the presbyters or only one called *episkopos*? This uncertainty holds for the New Testament and for some of the earliest post-New Testament Christian documents.

Ignatius of Antioch and Church Authority

The first clear expression of a distinction between the two levels of office in the local community is to be found in the letters of the martyr Ignatius of Antioch writing c.112 A.D. In these letters it is made abundantly clear that there is one officer of the local church who is its leader and head, the bishop. The presbyters are a collectivity subordinate to him. Reading his authentic letters, it is difficult not to have the impression that he is strongly urging the institution of a strong single leader on his audience (rather than taking it for granted as a universally accepted institution in place). Ignatius, concerned about the centrifugal forces present in many communities, the heresies and dissensions which tend to pull communities apart and destroy them, urges the need for a strong leader who gives commands, makes decisions, and clearly delineates the boundaries of the congregation gathered around him. For centuries, and indeed still at the present time, many scholars have been very slow to accept the authenticity of the letters of Ignatius precisely because they find it difficult to accept a full-blown doctrine of the monarchical episcopate at such an early date. They look to a much longer period of development before the monarchical bishop clearly becomes the rule in the Church by the end of the second century. Even if we accept the Ignatian views as authentically from the early second century, this does not prove by any means the existence of precisely that office or the same view of the office in the rest of the Church c.112 A.D.

The final element we should include in our study of the basic ingredients, which will ultimately combine to form a theory of doctrinal authority, is a very basic one. Even if one can determine historically a link between the founding Apostle of a given Christian community and its present episcopal leader, does that in itself prove the authority of the current leader? Here the earlier letter of the Roman community to the Church at Corinth is important. This work, called the *First Letter of Clement*, addressed the Corinthian community which had been torn asunder internally by elements which rejected the leadership of its presbyters. Using various scriptural examples, Clement argued that the presbyters ruled by God's will, and dissidents had no right to eject them. At one point, (c.42), Clement expressed the basic principle of apostolic succession. As the Father sent Christ, Christ sent the Apostles and they in turn selected the leaders of the local communities they founded. This principle established what sociologists would call the legitimacy of the ministry and authority of the leaders of the local church at any given moment in history. So long as they were not usurpers, the leaders of the local church were linked through a lengthening chain back to the Apostles and to Christ. This was not just an historical phenomenon, but one willed by God in his plan. These leaders then were the lawful holders of authority and preachers of the word.

Collegiality and Councils

All the basic elements had fallen into place by the late second century: the idea of a revelation now closed, given totally once and for all; a group of leaders of local churches with links, both historical and mystical, to the founding Apostles and thus through them to Christ and God. These leaders, then, are endowed with a quasi-divine authority. By the end of the second century, the leader in each community is clearly a monarchical bishop. These bishops and their public teaching are the ones to be consulted about the teaching of Christ. The bishops above all are the ones who must take care to teach a unified doctrine.

The Church had grown quickly and impressively. With growth came new problems, disputes which could not be solved within the narrow confines of a local church. There had always been in these communities, even under the strong episcopal leadership described by Ignatius of Antioch, an element of consultation and collegial decision-making. Thus it is not surprising that, from an early date, groups of Christian leaders from local churches met to discuss and seek solutions for increasingly knotty problems.

In matters that transcended local authority, councils were the means by which the leaders of the local churches could seek to solve questions that went beyond the boundaries of the local churches. The early Church seemed especially attracted to this means of solving problems. Even before the time of Constantine (306-337) the African Church, in particular, was attached to this collegial form of general governance. After the end of the persecutions, when travel was made easier for Christian bishops, larger and more frequent councils became a possibility. (Pagans complained that the imperial postal service was being ruined because it was constantly occupied in carrying Christian bishops from one council to another!) Constantine seemed to hit upon these councils with their larger complements of bishops as the ideal way to solve the questions which were agitating the Church (Donatism; Arianism) and threatening to tear it apart to the detriment of the empire. Thus we have the large councils of Arles (314) in the West and Nicaea (325) in the East, the latter traditionally considered as the first ecumenical (world) council. As we shall see, the Arian controversy, together with the imperial presence it helped call forth, generated so many contradictory councils in the fourth century that the authority of councils in general was endangered and probably inevitably lessened.

To a great extent the success of collegiality depended on the support of the emperor for the decisions reached by councils. Also vital was the agreement of the principal sees. In the Eastern empire, the leading sees were Alexandria and Antioch, the two largest cities. Their churches claimed foundation in New Testament times. Thus Hegesippus, the Jewish Christian traveller of the second century, had visited numerous churches of apostolic origin in the East in his struggle against Gnosticism. The emergence of Constantinople as New Rome in the fourth century brought a new and serious complication to this picture. In the East apostolic foundation by itself had never been the exclusive criterion for the significance of a church. For example, Alexandria had been the greatest city of the Greek world long before the legendary evangelization of the city by St. Mark. Constantinople did not (until much later) claim apostolic foundation. Its importance as a church lay in its position as an imperial capital. With the gradual eclipse of Alexandria and Antioch, it emerged as the New Rome of the Eastern Church as well as of the Eastern empire. While the Church as a whole came to regard consensus in one form or another as the ultimate state which overcame disputes, the Eastern Church looked upon the consensus of the principal sees of Rome, Constantinople, Alexandria, Antioch and Jerusalem as the key to the consensus of the whole Church.

Over against this Eastern view, Rome, the sole apostolic see of the West, came to regard itself as superior to the other sees, including the great Eastern churches, not because of political, historical or even canonical reasons but because of divine ordinance. From the mid-fourth century, when our evidence becomes abundant, it is clear that the Roman see considered itself to hold a special, indeed pre-eminent, place in the battle to preserve undistorted the apostolic message. Thus we find two divergent tendencies, the one, especially strong in the East, that looked to consensus and reception as the ultimate criteria in doctrinal questions. Here the general council would be the supreme expression of this consensus with the emperor enforcing its decisions. The Roman see came to view itself as superior to councils, that its tradition was apostolic without taint and therefore normative for the Church as a whole. It sought less to conform itself to a general consensus, even one formed at a council, than to impose its views on the Church as a whole, to impose a consensus more or less from above.

Chapter One

THE SECOND CENTURY

Oral Tradition
Papias of Hierapolis

According to tradition, Papias was bishop of Hierapolis in Asia Minor in the early second century. Only fragments of his writings remain. Papias boasts of his contacts with men of the first century. He prides himself on his reliance on the oral tradition. But we ought to see in him rather a witness to the problems of relying on oral traditions. The variations in the oral traditions gave rise to the need for written documents; finally, the multiplication of written documents pointed up the need for selection and led to the notion of a canon of the New Testament. Eusebius, the historian, clearly had a low opinion of Papias. The reason for this was Papias' espousal of a literal millenarianism.

EUSEBIUS OF CAESAREA, CHURCH HISTORY

On Papias

III. 39[1] (Quoting Irenaeus) "Papias, who heard John and was a companion of Polycarp, a man of the olden days, has given written testimony in the fourth of his books. In all, he wrote five books." (Cf. *Against Heresies*, V.33.4). So much for Irenaeus.

[1]Text: SC 31.153-156.

However, Papias in the preface to his books does not prove ever to have personally heard or seen the holy Apostles. But he learned what he did know from people who had known the Apostles. Here are his own words:

"On your behalf, I will not hesitate to add to my own explanations what I learned formerly from the elders. I have kept these recollections to strengthen the truth. For I did not particularly care for those who talk a lot as most do but I was interested in those who teach the truth; nor did I care for those who taught alien commands but rather for those who recalled the commandments given by the Lord to the faith and sprung from the truth itself. Whenever someone who had been a follower of the elders came along, I made a special effort to hear the words of the elders, what Andrew or Peter had said, Philip, Thomas, James or John, Matthew or any of the Lord's disciples; also what Aristion said or John the Elder, disciples of the Lord. I did not think that what came from books was as important as what came from the living and abiding voice."

The same Papias adds other things which came to him through some oral tradition, some strange parables of the Saviour and certain odd teachings and other completely unfounded things. For example, he says that there will be a thousand years after the Resurrection of the dead and that the reign of Christ will be realized in a material way on earth. I think that he got all this from a misunderstanding of what the Apostles wrote because he did not grasp that they should be interpreted symbolically and figuratively. All in all, he does not appear to have been very bright, as you will see if you look at his books.

The Development of Church Office

THE TEACHING OF THE TWELVE APOSTLES (THE *DIDACHE*)

One of the important components in the development of doctrinal authority is the question: Who decides? And this in turn is very much involved with the question of Church office. The development of Church office itself has long been a subject of controversy. The present arrangement of bishop, priest and deacon developed in the first and second centuries until it became universal in the late second century. The *Didache* or "Teaching of the Twelve Apostles" is a document, probably Syrian, whose origins go back to the first century. That part of the document which deals with Church office is principally concerned with a form of itinerant ministry of Apostles, prophets and teachers. It seems to represent a transitional period because it also mentions the beginnings of a local, stable ministry of bishops and deacons. The *Didache* finds it necessary to bolster their position in the face of popular skepticism.

The Didache
15[2] Therefore, ordain for yourselves bishops and deacons worthy of the Lord, meek men, not avaricious, truthful, chosen. They will also fulfill for you the work of the prophets and teachers. Do not look down on them, for they should be honored by you along with the prophets and teachers.

IGNATIUS OF ANTIOCH

Ignatius is known only from the seven letters he wrote while being taken by the imperial authorities from Antioch to Rome to die a martyr's death in the early second century. Ignatius wrote to the local churches in Western Asia Minor which helped him on his journey. For the first time, these letters show the distinct Church offices of bishop, presbyter and deacon, with the single bishop as the undisputed leader of the local community. This early

[2]Text: SC 248.192-194.

appearance of the monepiscopate has caused continuing debate about the authenticity and dating of these letters. There is further discussion as to whether or not the monepiscopate was already well established and accepted, or whether Ignatius is to be seen as the archprotagonist of this form of leadership. He clearly sees obedience to the bishop and centralizing trends as the principal weapon against the centrifugal forces of heresy which threaten to pull the Church apart. There is no particular emphasis on apostolic succession.

The Letter to the Ephesians

4.[3] It is fitting that you walk in accord with the thought of your bishop, as you are doing. Your justly known presbyterium, worthy of God, is fitted to the bishop as strings to a harp; thus, in your harmonious love, Jesus Christ is being sung. May each of you also become a member of the choir, so that in harmonious unity, taking the pitch from God in unison, you may sing through Jesus Christ with a single voice to the Father so that he may hear you and recognize you through your good works as members of his Son. It is useful for you to live in perfect unity so that you may continue to participate in God.

5. If I in so short a time have become so close to your bishop in an intimacy that is entirely spiritual and not merely human, how much more blessed is it for you to be closely united to him as the Church is to Jesus Christ, and Jesus to the Father, so that all things agree in harmonious unity. Let no one wander off; if anyone is not within the sanctuary he is depriving himself of the bread of God. For if the prayer of one or two people together has so much power, how much greater the united prayer of bishop and congregation. Anyone who spurns the liturgical assembly shows himself arrogant and judges himself, as it is written, "God resists the proud." (Prv 3.34) Let us then take care not to

[3]Text: SC 10.72-74.

stand against the bishop so that we will be submissive to God...

6. So it is clear that we must look upon the bishop as the Lord himself.

The Letter to the Magnesians

6.[4] Since in the visitors I have mentioned above, I have seen in faith and loved your entire community, so I beg you, take great care always to act in God's concord, with the bishop who holds the place of God, with the presbyters, who are like the college of the Apostles, and with the deacons who are so dear to me, to whom Jesus' own special work has been entrusted... Let there be nothing among you to serve as an excuse for schism, but unite yourselves to the bishop and to those who preside as an example and lesson of immortality.

7. Just as the Lord did nothing either by himself or through his Apostles without his Father, with whom he is one, so you should do nothing without the bishops and the presbyters. Do not try to make what you do on your own look acceptable but always act with others: a single prayer, a single petition, one mind, one hope in love, in joy beyond reproach: This is Jesus Christ to whom nothing is to be preferred. All of you hasten to come together as in a single temple of God, around a single altar, united with the one Jesus Christ....

The Letter to the Trallians

2.[5] For when you submit to the bishop as to Jesus Christ, I see you living, not as men live, but as Jesus Christ, who died for you, wants. Believing in his death, you escape death. You must do nothing without the bishop, as indeed you do. You must also submit to the presbyterium as to the Apostles of Jesus Christ, our hope...

7. Keep yourselves from people like that (i.e. heretics).

[4]Text: SC 10. 98-100
[5]Text: SC 10. 112,116

You will succeed if you remain inseparable from Jesus Christ in God and from the bishop and the commands of the Apostles. The person within the sanctuary is pure but the person who is outside is not; i.e. he who acts without the bishop, presbyters and deacons, is the one whose conscience is not clear.

The Letter to the Philadelphians

3.[6] Keep yourselves from harmful plants which Jesus Christ does not raise because they were not planted by the Father. What I found among you was not schism but a sort of weeding out process. All those who belong to God and Jesus Christ are with the bishop. All those who repent and come back to the unity of the Church, these will also be God's that they may live according to Jesus Christ. "Do not be deceived," brothers, if anyone promotes schism, "he will have no part in the Kingdom of God." (I Cor 6.8-10) If anyone follows an alien faith, he is not in agreement with the Passion of Christ.

4. Be very careful to participate in a single Eucharist: for there is only one flesh of our Lord Jesus Christ and a single cup by which we are united in his blood, a single altar and a single bishop with the presbyters and deacons, my fellow servants. Whatever you do, do it God's way.

The Letter to the Smyrnaeans

8.[7] Follow the bishop, all of you, as Jesus Christ follows his Father, and the presbyterium as the Apostles. As for the deacons, respect them as the Law of God. Let no one do anything with reference to the Church without the bishop. Only that Eucharist may be regarded as legitimate which is celebrated with the bishop or his delegate presiding. Where the bishop is, there let the community be, just as where Jesus Christ is, there is the Catholic Church. Without the bishop, you are allowed neither to baptize nor to hold an *agape*

[6]Text: SC 10. 142-144
[7]Text: SC 10. 162-164

celebration. Whatever he approves is fine in God's sight so that all that is done may be legitimized and certain.

9. It is reasonable to start being sensible again and, while there is still time, to repent and come back to God. It is good to honor God and the bishop. The one who honors the bishop will be honored by God. The one who does something and hides it from the bishop serves the Devil.

Apostolic Succession

THE FIRST LETTER OF CLEMENT OF ROME

Clement is traditionally considered the third bishop of Rome after Peter. There is some question about the precise form of the leadership of the Roman Christian community in the first and second centuries. It can be said, at least, that Clement played a significant role in the late first century. Once many writings were attributed to Clement; now only this letter is still regarded as his, though, ironically, his name is never mentioned in the text tradition.

This is a letter from the community of the Roman Christians to the community of the Corinthian Christians calling upon the latter to return to order after some problem concerning their presbyters had ruptured their unity. The letter bases the authority of the community's leaders on what would later be called "apostolic succession." It seeks to establish a link between Christ, the Apostles and later generations of Church leaders. By so doing it hopes to legitimize the authority of Church leaders and thus protect them from undue pressure within the community. However, it does not give evidence of the existence of the monepiscopate either in Rome or in Corinth. The odd Old Testament citation at the end of the selection is a variation on the Septuagint (Greek) version of Isaiah 60.17.

42.[8] The Apostles first received the Gospel for us from the Lord Jesus Christ; Jesus the Christ was sent by God. Thus the Christ comes from God; the Apostles from the Christ; both have issued in due order from the will of God. They received instructions and, filled with certitude by the resurrection of our Lord Jesus Christ, fortified by the word of God, filled with certainty by the Holy Spirit, they set out to announce the Good News that the Kingdom of God was coming. They preached in the countryside and in towns and they tested in the Spirit their first converts in order to make of them bishops and deacons for those who would later come to believe. And there was nothing new about this: for long ago, Scripture spoke of bishops and deacons. Somewhere in Scripture there appear the following words: "I will appoint their bishops in justice and their deacons in faith." (Is 60.17 LXX)

Apostolic Succession and Tradition

THE PSEUDO-CLEMENTINE LITERATURE: THE LETTER OF PETER TO JAMES

> The so-called pseudo-Clementines are a group of writings formerly attributed to Clement of Rome. Today they are usually attributed to Jewish-Christian circles in which an important leadership role was assigned to James of Jerusalem, portrayed as a traditionalist leader opposed to the Pauline minimizing of the Jewish Law. This excerpt from an apocryphal letter of Peter stresses the need for vigilance concerning tradition. It also smacks of the idea of an esoteric tradition.

3.[9] In order that such things not be repeated (i.e. the misrepresenting of Peter's teaching), I think it a good idea and I hereby ask that you do not give the books of my preaching which I sent you to anyone, neither of our race

[8]Text: SC 167.168-170
[9]Text: GCS 42^2. 2

nor of any other, unless he first be tested and found trust-
worthy. If so, then give them to him as Moses did when he
gave (his books) to the Seventy who succeeded to his chair
of teaching so that they may guard the articles of faith and
everywhere transmit the rule of the truth, explaining all
things according to our tradition, lest they, being overcome
by ignorance or led astray by their personal theories, may
lead others into the same pit of perdition.

HEGESIPPUS (IN) EUSEBIUS, CHURCH HISTORY

Hegesippus was a Jewish Christian writer of the second
century. Faced with the divisive threat from Gnosticism,
Hegesippus says that he travelled about, comparing the
teachings of the local churches, especially those founded
by Apostles. He found a uniformity of teaching contrasted with the contradictory teachings of the various
Gnostic masters. Hegesippus is important because of his
emphasis on the historical verification of the link of the
teaching of the apostolic sees with the teaching of Christ
and the Apostles through the *diadochai*, successions of
bishops.

IV.22[10] In the five books of his *Memoirs* which have
survived, Hegesippus has left us a very complete record of
his own ideas. He tells us that he visited a great many
bishops, sailing as far as Rome and, in addition, that he
heard the same teaching from every one of them. It will be
good to hear his own words on this... "And the church of
the Corinthians remained orthodox up to the time Primus
became bishop of Corinth. We spent some days with them
during which we were encouraged by their orthodoxy.
When I was at Rome, I made a succession (list) up to the
time of Anicetus. Eleutherus was his deacon; Soter succeeded Anicetus and after him, came Eleutherus. In each
succession and in each city, you will find things as they
should be, as the Law, the Prophets and the Lord have
preached."

[10]Text: SC 31. 199-200

A Conflict of Traditions: The Quartodeciman Controversy

While the related issues — the day on which the Lord's Resurrection is to be celebrated and the fast is to end — are not of direct interest here, the controversy does illustrate the problem of reconciling differing ancient traditions found in various parts of the world Church. The incident also shows the early use of regional councils to settle controversies and furnishes as well an example of Roman intervention, though the explanation of the latter is disputed. We see both Roman insistence on uniformity and episcopal indignation that a certain degree of overkill is being exercised.

EUSEBIUS, CHURCH HISTORY

V.23[11] In those days, a question of some importance was raised because the churches of the whole province of Asia, following a very ancient tradition, thought that they should keep the fourteenth day of the moon as the feast of the Lord's Pasch. This was the day on which the Jews immolated the Lamb, and according to them, it was absolutely necessary on whatever day of the week that that date fell, to end the fast then. But the churches of the rest of the world did not have the custom of observing this way of doing things and according to the apostolic tradition they kept the usage still in possession up to now, thinking it not right to end the fast any other day than on the day of the Lord's Resurrection.

Synods and assemblies of bishops were called on this question. All with one accord promulgated an ecclesiastical decree for the faithful everywhere, deciding that the mystery of the Lord's Resurrection from the dead would never be celebrated any other day but Sunday and on that day only should we end the Holy Week fast.

There is still extant a letter from those who assembled in

[11]Text: SC 41. 66

Palestine over whom presided Theophilus, bishop of Caesarea, and Narcissus, bishop of Jerusalem. Similarly, there is another letter on the same question from those gathered in Rome. It shows that Victor was bishop there; another from the bishops of Pontus where Palmas as senior bishop presided; still another from the churches of Gaul where Irenaeus was bishop; another from the bishops of Osrhoene and the cities of that region and especially from Bacchyllus, bishop of Corinth, and from a great many others. They all have the same opinion and make the same decision with the same decree...

V.24[12] But the bishops of the province of Asia affirmed forcefully that they had to keep the ancient primitive custom which had been handed down to them. They were led by Polycrates. In the letter he wrote to Victor and the Roman church, he explained their traditional observance in the following terms:

"We celebrate with scrupulous care this day, taking nothing away and adding nothing. Here in Asia repose great luminaries who will rise on the day of the Lord's return ... Philip, one of the twelve Apostles, who reposes at Hierapolis with his two daughters who grew old as virgins; his other daughter who lived in the Holy Spirit reposes at Ephesus. And John also, who lay his head on the Lord's breast, who was a priest wearing the golden breastplate, martyr and teacher, he reposes at Ephesus; also Polycarp of Smyrna, bishop and martyr: and Thraseas of Eumenaea, bishop and martyr who reposes at Smyrna. Need we speak of Sagaris, bishop and martyr, who reposes at Laodicaea and blessed Papias and the eunuch Melito who lived entirely in the Holy Spirit, who reposes at Sardis, awaiting the Lord's return at which he will raise the dead? All of these observed the fourteenth day of the Pasch, (i.e. they were Quartodecimans) according to the Gospel, not transgressing but conforming themselves to the rule of faith.

As for myself, I am the least of all of you. I, Polycrates,

[12]Text: SC 41. 67-69

live according to the tradition of those of my family, some of whom I have followed. Seven of my family were bishops; I am the eighth. And all of them observed the day when the people abstain from leavened bread. As for myself, my brother, I am sixty-five years old in the Lord and have had contacts with brethren all over the world. I have searched all the Scriptures. I am not frightened by those who threaten me, for greater men than I have said: 'We must obey God rather than men.' (Acts 5.29)"

He added to this a propos of the bishops who were with him when he wrote and who were of the same opinion: "I could mention the bishops with me whom you asked me to call together, and I did so. Their names, if I were to write them all down, would be very numerous. They, well aware of my faltering courage, approved my letter, knowing that I am not grey-haired for nothing but that I have always lived in Christ Jesus."

After this, the head of the Roman church, Victor, undertook to cut off from the common unity the churches of the whole province of Asia *en masse* — as well as some of the neighboring churches for being heterodox. He sent out letters and proclaimed that all the brethren in those places without exception were excommunicated. But this did not please all the bishops. They advised him to have a greater concern for peace, for unity and charity. Their words are still known; they blamed Victor rather sharply.

Chapter Two

AN INITIAL SYNTHESIS: IRENAEUS OF LYON

Apostolic Tradition — Episcopal Succession
The Rule of Faith

Irenaeus was bishop of Lyon (Lugdunum) in the late second century. He is one of the earliest and most significant of Christian theologians. His principal surviving work, *Against Heresies*, was aimed against the Gnostics and has long been an essential source for their teachings. In opposition, he states the Christian Rule of Faith, giving the content of the apostolic faith as taught by the Church. In his refutation of the Gnostics, he appeals to the teachings of the apostolic churches. The Roman church is for him the outstanding example among these ancient churches. Thus the person seeking the apostolic teaching should look to what is publicly taught and handed down in these churches.

The Gnostics also claimed some sort of hidden chain of succession or witnesses linking them with an Apostle (usually one of the more obscure ones!). In fact, argued Irenaeus, the individual Gnostic teachers disproved their own claims by the fact that each master contradicted his own predecessors as well as rival teachers. In contrast, the churches were united in their proclamation.

AGAINST HERESIES

I.10.1[1] The Church, although scattered throughout the earth to its very limits, received from the Apostles and their disciples this faith: There is one God, the Father almighty "who made heaven and earth and the sea and all they contain." (Acts 4.24;14.15) (We believe) in one Christ Jesus, the Son of God, who became flesh for our salvation, and in the Holy Spirit who announced God's plan through the Prophets: his coming, his birth from the Virgin, his passion and resurrection from the dead, the ascension in the flesh to heaven of his beloved Jesus Christ our Lord and his return from Heaven in the glory of the Father to gather all things and to raise in the flesh the entire human race so that to Christ Jesus, our Lord and God, Savior and King, according to the good pleasure of the invisible Father, "every knee must bend in the heavens and on earth and under the earth and every tongue confess him" (Phil. 2.10-11). He will render a just judgment on all, sending into eternal fire all the wicked spirits who became sinful, apostate angels as well as evil, blaspheming human beings. On the other side, he will bestow eternal life and endless glory on the just, on those who keep his commandments and persevere in his love, some from the very beginning, others, after repentance.

I.10.2 The Church, having received this message and this faith, now spread throughout the whole world, carefully guards it as if dwelling in one house and believes the same things as if it had one soul and one heart. It preaches, teaches and hands on all this in harmonious unity as if it had but one mouth. For although there are in the world many diverse forms of speech, yet the force of the tradition is one and the same. Nor do churches founded in Germany believe or teach otherwise, nor do those among the Iberians, among the Celts, in the East, in Egypt, in Libya, nor those established in the center of the world. Just as the sun, God's creature, is one and the same throughout the world, so the light, the preaching of the truth, shines everywhere and

[1]Text: SC 264. 154-160

illuminates everyone who is willing to come to the knowledge of the truth. Neither will the eloquent man among the Church's leaders preach anything other than this, for no one is above his master, nor will the person who is not very capable weaken the tradition. Since it is one and the same faith, it cannot be expanded by someone who says much, any more than it can be diminished by one who says little.

I.22.1[2] For us who keep the Rule of Truth, there is one God the almighty who created all things through his Word, who fashioned all things and made all things out of that which did not exist, just as the Scripture says: "By the Word of the Lord, the heavens were made; by the breath of his mouth all their host." (Ps 33.6) and again: "All things were made by him and without him nothing was made." (Jn 1.3). There are no exceptions to this created totality, but through him the Father made everything, whether visible or invisible, whether perceived by the senses or only by the mind, whether temporal because of some plan or eternal. He did not create all these things by means of angels or powers somehow detached from his will, for God has no need of anything. Rather through his Word and Spirit he makes all things, guides all things and gives all things continued existence. He made the world, for the "world" means all the things he created. He fashioned man. This is the God of Abraham, the God of Isaac and the God of Jacob, above whom there is no other God, or Beginning, or Virtue, or Pleroma. He is the Father of our Lord Jesus Christ, as we shall demonstrate. We keep this rule and thus we can show easily that they, however diverse and numerous their words, have wandered from the truth. For almost all the heresies, numerous as they are, speak of one God, but they change (him) by their evil teaching, ungrateful as they are toward him who made them. They are no different from the pagans and their idols. They scorn God's handiwork, overturning their own salvation; these people are most bitter accusers and false witnesses. Indeed they will rise in the flesh, however unwilling, as they do not know the power of him who

[2]Text: SC 264. 308-310

raises them from the dead; hence they shall not be numbered among the just because of their lack of faith.

III.3.1[3] The tradition of the Apostles is there, manifest throughout the world in each church, to be seen by all who wish to see the truth. Further we can list those who were appointed by the Apostles to be bishops in the churches and their successors to our own day. What they taught and what they knew had nothing to do with these (Gnostic) absurdities. Still, even if the Apostles had known hidden mysteries which they taught the "perfect" apart from the rest, surely they would have passed on such knowledge above all to those to whom they entrusted the churches. For they wished the men whom they designated as successors and to whom they left their teaching office to be perfect and beyond reproach in all things. So, if these men were to accomplish their task faultlessly, it would be a great gain, but, if not, the greatest disaster.

III.3.2 But since it would be extremely long in a book such as this to give the succession lists for all the churches (we shall take just one), the greatest and most ancient church, known to all, founded at Rome by the two most glorious apostles, Peter and Paul. We shall show that its tradition, which it has from the Apostles and the faith preached to men, comes down to us through the succession of bishops. Thus we shall confound all who, in whatever way, either through self-satisfaction or vainglory, blindness or doctrinal error, form communities they should not. For every church, i.e. the faithful who are in all parts of the world, should agree with this church because of its superior foundation. In this church the tradition from the Apostles has been preserved by those who are from all parts of the world.

III.3.3 The blessed Apostles after founding and providing for the church, handed over the leadership and care of the church to Linus (the same one Paul mentioned in his letters to Timothy; cf. 2 Tm 4.21). Anacletus succeeded him. Next, in the third place from the Apostles, Clement received the episcopate, a man who had seen the Apostles themselves

[3]Text: SC 211. 30-44

and had talked with them. He still had their preaching resounding in his ears and their teaching before his eyes. He was not the only one, of course. At that time there still survived many who had been taught by the Apostles. It was during the time of this Clement that no small dissension arose among the brethren in Corinth. The church of Rome wrote a most powerful letter to the Corinthians, calling them back to peace, restoring their faith, and proclaiming to them the tradition recently received from the Apostles, that there is one God Almighty, the maker of Heaven and Earth, the fashioner of man, who brought about the deluge, called Abraham, who led the people from the land of Egypt, who spoke with Moses, who gave the Law and sent the prophets, who prepared fire for the Devil and his angels. That this God is the Father of our Lord Jesus Christ is preached by the churches. All who wish to learn can do so from this very letter and they can understand the apostolic tradition of the Church since the letter is older than those who now teach falsely and invent another God who is above the Demiurge and Creator of all things.

To this Clement succeeded Evaristus; to Evaristus, Alexander, and then, sixth from the Apostles, Sixtus. After him came Telesphorus who gloriously suffered martyrdom. And then Hyginus; afterwards Pius, and after him, Anicetus. After Soter succeeded Anicetus, then came Eleutherus who now holds the episcopate, the twelfth from the Apostles. By this order and succession, the tradition of the Apostles in the Church and the preaching of the truth have come down to us. And this is a most complete demonstration that one and the same life-giving faith which is in the Church from the Apostles until now has been preserved and handed down in truth.

III.3.4 And Polycarp also, who not only was taught by the Apostles and lived with many of those who had seen our Lord, but was also made bishop of the Church at Smyrna by the Apostles in Asia, this very man we once saw in our childhood. He lived a long life and as a very old man most gloriously and nobly suffered martyrdom, departing this life. He always taught these things and that they alone are the truth. All the churches in Asia and those who up until now have succeeded Polycarp bear witness to these (teachings). Polycarp was a much greater authority and more faithful witness to the truth than Valentinus and Marcion and all the other teachers of perverse doctrines.

For when Polycarp, in the time of Anicetus, came to Rome, by his preaching he brought back many of the heretics to the Church of God, proclaiming that he had received from the Apostles one truth and one only, the very same which he himself passed on to the Church. And there are some who heard him tell the story of John, the disciple of the Lord. Going to the baths one day in Ephesus, when he saw Cerinthus inside, he ran from the baths without bathing, saying that he was afraid the building might collapse since Cerinthus, the enemy of the truth, was inside. And Polycarp himself once met Marcion who said to him: "You know me." He answered: "I know you, the first-born of Satan." Such great fear did the Apostles and their disciples have lest they communicate even by a word with one of those who had perverted the truth... There is also the church at Ephesus, founded by Paul, where John remained up until the time of Trajan, a true witness to the tradition of the Apostles.

III.4.1[4] So forceful are these arguments that no one should henceforth seek the truth from any other source since it is so simple to get it from the Church. The Apostles, like rich men with a treasure, have brought to the Church the whole of the truth so that anyone at all who wishes can come and take from it the elixir of life. This is the gateway to life; all others are thieves and robbers. Hence all those are to be avoided. But, on the contrary, we are to love the things of the Church with the greatest zeal and to take hold of the tradition of the truth. What then? If there arise a dispute about some question of moderate significance, should we not have recourse to the most ancient churches, in which the Apostles carried on their work and on this question take from them what is clear and certain? What if the Apostles

[4]Text: SC 211. 44-48

had not left us the Scriptures, would it not be necessary to follow the order of tradition which they handed down to those to whom they entrusted the churches?

III.4.2. It is to that order (of Tradition) that many barbarian nations who believe in Christ assent, possessing their salvation written in their hearts by the Spirit without paper and ink, and zealously keeping to the old tradition. They believe in one God, the Creator of Heaven and Earth and all things in them, and in Christ Jesus, the Son of God, who because of his outstanding love for his handiwork, agreed to be engendered by the Virgin so that he might in his own person unite man to God. He suffered under Pontius Pilate, rose, was taken up into glory and will return in glory, the Savior of those who are saved and the Judge of those who are to be judged, sending into eternal fire those who have distorted the truth and showed contempt for his father and for his own incarnation. This faith they have believed although illiterate; in comparison to our language they are barbarians. But as for their beliefs, their customs and their way of life, because of this faith they are wise and pleasing to God. They live lives of justice, chastity and wisdom.

If anyone should preach to them the things invented by heretics, even speaking to them in their own tongue, they would run away, shutting their ears, not willing to listen to such blasphemous talk. Because of that ancient tradition coming from the Apostles, they are unwilling to consider even for a second any of their absurd teachings.

III.24.1[5] By way of contrast, the preaching of the Church presents a message that is in every place, and at each moment, consistent and unchanging. The prophets and Apostles and all the disciples bear witness to it. It encompasses the beginning, the end, and the whole of history, the entirety of God's plan for the world, everything which works toward the accomplishment of human salvation — in short, our faith. Having received it from the Church, we keep it safe. It is the precious, life-giving deposit kept in a lovely

[5]Text: SC 211. 470-474

and secure place, which through the Spirit of God renews the youth even of its guardians.

This gift of God has been entrusted to the Church, just as breath in God's creation, so that all the members receiving it may be given life; and in it you find communion with Christ, i.e. the Holy Spirit, the pledge of immortality, the confirming of our faith, and the stairway for climbing up to God. "In the Church," he says, "God has placed Apostles, prophets, teachers" (I Cor 12.28) and the entire activity of the Spirit. Those who do not come to the Church do not share in his grace but deprive themselves of life by their evil doctrines and works. For where the Church is, there is the Spirit of God; and where the Spirit is, there is the Church and all grace, for the Spirit is truth. Therefore those who do not partake of the Spirit are not nourished by the breasts of Mother Church unto life, nor do they receive sustenance from the clear spring flowing from Christ's body but they dig for themselves "broken cisterns" (Jer 2.13), holes in the earth, and they drink filthy water from the sewer, fleeing the faith of the Church lest they be exposed and rejecting the Spirit lest they be instructed.

III.24.2 Alienated from the truth, they wallow in every error, tossed about, as time goes by, by one opinion one day and another, the next. With no firm teaching, they prefer to be known for their clever words rather than for being disciples of truth. They are not built on a rock, but on sand, sand with lots of stones.

IV.25.3[6] Patriarchs and prophets sowed the word concerning Christ and the Church harvested it, i.e. gathered the fruit...

IV.26.1 If, then, someone reads the Scriptures in this way, he will find there a word concerning Christ and a prefiguring of the new calling. For he is "the treasure hidden in the field" (Mt 13.44), i.e. in the world, since "the field is the world" (Mt 13.38). The treasure was hidden in the Scriptures, for it was symbolized by the figures and parables which, humanly

[6]Text: SC 100. 71-72

speaking, could not have been understood before the fulfillment of the prophecies, i.e. before the coming of the
Lord... This is why the Law, when read by the Jews in our
own time, seems like a fable: for they lack that which is the
explanation of the whole thing, i.e. the coming of the Son of
God as man. On the contrary, when read by Christians, this
is the treasure hidden in the field, revealed and explained by
the cross of Christ. It enriches human understanding, shows
the wisdom of God, helps us to understand God's plan for
man. It prefigures the kingdom of Christ and proclaims in
advance the good news of the inheritance of holy Jerusalem.
It tells us that the one who loves God will come to the vision
of God and will hear his word and by hearing it, will be
glorified to such a degree that others will not be able to look
upon his glorious face... If you read the Scriptures in this
way...you will be a perfect disciple.

IV.26.2 Wherefore you must listen to those who are elders
in the Church, those who hold the succession from the
Apostles, as we have shown, who, together with the succession of the episcopate, have received the certain charism of
truth. But the rest, those who depart from the original
succession and gather apart — these must be considered
suspect either of being heretics, or of wrong ideas, or as
schismatics, proud and self-satisfied, or as hypocrites working for money or fame. All of these stray from the truth.

IV.26.4 You must turn away from all men like this. On the
contrary, stay close to those who, as we have said, maintain
the succession of the Apostles and in the order of presbyters,
of the sound teaching and irreproachable conduct as a good
example for the reform of others.

Chapter Three

PROPAGATING THE SYNTHESIS: TERTULLIAN OF CARTHAGE

Tertullian is the first great Latin theologian. A master polemicist, Tertullian was also an extremist. He was converted to Christianity c.194 in Carthage but within a few years he joined the Montanist sect which maintained a rigoristic stance. Tertullian developed the arguments advanced by Irenaeus in a clear, forceful and succinct fashion. In particular, his treatise *The Prescription against the Heretics* (c.203) sought to rule out in advance all heretical claims on the ground that only the Church rightfully possessed the Scriptures. Ironically Tertullian later left the Church. When reproached with his own arguments, he replied that he was not inconsistent at all, that he had advocated no change in the rule of faith but only a greater strictness in discipline. His final writings date to about 221.

AGAINST PRAXEAS

Tertullian made significant contributions to several areas of theology, including the theology of the Trinity. In his *Against Praxeas*, he notes the mutual lack of understanding which even then caused friction between theologians and ordinary Christians. In this case, since Christians prided themselves on being monotheists, they sometimes had difficulties in understanding the idea of a Trinity of co-equal persons.

3.[1] The simple believers, not to speak of the ignorant and uneducated, always comprise the majority of the faithful. Since the rule of faith itself has brought them from the many gods of the world to the one true God, they do not comprehend that belief in the divine unity must be linked with the divine economy and are thus frightened away by the economy. They presume that the trinitarian number and arrangement mean a loss of unity, whereas in fact the unity, out of which is derived the Trinity, is not destroyed by it but is simply arranged into a certain order. Thus people object that I preach two or three gods, while, they say, they are worshippers of only one God, as if unity unreasonably compressed, would not result in heresy, and a Trinity, sensibly measured, constitute the truth. They say: We are sticking with the Monarchy. And thus even the Latins make the sound of that word. They do it so well, you might get the idea that they understood the meaning of 'monarchy' as well as they pronounce it...

THE FLESH OF CHRIST

> In his treatise on the Incarnation, *The Flesh of Christ*, Tertullian battles an old adversary, Marcion, who, among other things, rejected the Old Testament and maintained that a real incarnation was unworthy of God. Tertullian argues that the incarnate Son of God was fully human; his flesh was quite real. He questions Marcion's authority to teach anything.

2.[2] By what authority, pray? Prove it. If you are a prophet, predict something. If you are an apostle, preach in public. If you are an apostolic man, agree with the Apostles. If you are an ordinary Christian, believe what has been handed down. If you are none of the above, then, with good reason I say: Drop dead! For you are already dead, you who are no Christian, not accepting the faith that makes us Chris-

---

[1]Text: CCL 2. 1161
[2]Text: CCL 2. 875

tians... What was handed down was true as it was handed down by those commissioned to do so. Thus, by rejecting what was handed down, you have rejected the truth. You had no right to do that.

BAPTISM; PURITY

The next two excerpts deal with the Canon of the New Testament. Tertullian accepts and rejects works as they support or undermine his own views. Here he rejects the *Acts of Paul* since they might be construed as giving support to the right of women to teach in church. In the second text, he accepts the letter to the Hebrews (with Barnabas as its author) because some passages seem sympathetic to rigorism. He rejects the apocryphal *Shepherd* of Hermas since it offers the possibility of forgiveness to post-baptismal sinners, including adulterers.

Baptism

17.[3] But if certain *Acts of Paul*, which were written under false pretences, are brought forward as defending the right of women to teach and baptize because of the example of Thecla, it should be known that it was a presbyter in the province of Asia who put it together, as if by his efforts he could make Paul greater. Having been found out and claiming he did it out of love for Paul, he was forced from his position.

Purity

(Scripture is in favor of strict discipline. Beyond this there is a writing of a companion of the Apostles.)

20.[4] For there is also a letter to the Hebrews, a work of Barnabas, a man sufficiently attested by God, a man whom Paul associated with himself in asceticism. "Is it only myself and Barnabas who are forced to work for a living?" (I Cor

[3]Text: CCL 1. 291-292
[4]Text: CCL 2.1324

9.6) And indeed this letter of Barnabas has had a much wider acceptance in the Church than the apocryphal *Shepherd* of adulterers.

EXHORTATION TO CHASTITY

In the *Exhortation to Chastity*, Tertullian argues that widowed Christians should not re-marry. In this excerpt, he answers the objection that such a discipline pertains only to the clergy. His argument that all Christians are priests by reason of their baptism has usually been rejected by Catholic commentators as an example of Montanist heresy. It is not clear that such an objection solves the problem. He does not deny the existence of a clerical hierarchy or even its fittingness. He simply asserts that necessity allows of exceptions to what is essentially an ecclesiastical rather than a divinely instituted order.

7.[5] But you may say: "Therefore this must be permitted to those whom he exempts. " We would certainly be foolish if we thought that what was not permitted to priests was permitted to laity. For are not we laity also priests? It is written: "He has made us a kingdom and priests for God and his Father." (Rv 1.6) It is the authority of the Church that instituted the distinction between clergy and laity and the honor shown the ranks of the clergy made holy for God. Where there is no duly constituted clergy, you offer, you baptize, you are your own priest, for where there are three, this is a church, albeit of laity.

For, as the apostle says, each one "lives by his faith; there is no respect of persons with God," (Heb 2.4; Rom 1.17) since "not the hearers, but the doers, of the Law are justified." (Rom 2.11) Therefore, if, in time of necessity, you yourself have the right to be a priest, it is necessary that you also maintain a priestly discipline even when it is not necessary for you to act as a priest. Do you, a remarried person, baptize? Do you offer? How much greater a sin is it for a

[5]Text: CCL 2. 1024-1025

remarried layman to act as a priest when the right to priestly ministry is withdrawn from a real priest who marries again. But, you may object, necessity knows no law. There can be no excuse for such an unnecessary "necessity." The simple solution is: do not remarry and, when a genuine necessity arises, you will have no problem. God wishes all of us to be ready at all times to administer the sacraments.

THE PRESCRIPTION AGAINST THE HERETICS

In the context of this book, Tertullian's most significant work is the *Prescription against the Heretics*. The 'prescription' in question pertains to law rather than medicine. Tertullian tries to counter every possible ploy of the Gnostics, e.g. that Christ did not tell all to his Apostles or that the Apostles did not tell all to their converts. Like Irenaeus, he rejects their claim to a special esoteric knowledge derived through a secret tradition from the Apostles, opposing it with the claim that the Apostles knew all there was to know of Jesus' teaching and passed it on intact and undiluted to the churches they founded. The churches in turn continue to teach this publicly to all willing to listen. The churches of historically apostolic origins are key here because they can offer in evidence an historical list of witnesses to their teaching, their bishops. The uniformity of the teaching of these churches around the world is a further counter to the babel of conflicting voices coming from the Gnostics. At the end of his work, Tertullian attacks the anarchy prevailing in the ranks of the heretics.

6.[6] (Paul warns Titus to beware of heresy.) . . . Heresy gets its name from the Greek word meaning "choice," a choice one exercises to the full either by spreading heresy or simply by adopting one. Therefore the heretic has proclaimed himself condemned since he has chosen the means of his own condemnation. We, on the other hand, are allowed to intro-

[6]Text: CCL 1. 191

duce nothing of our own invention nor to choose a product of someone else's choice. For us the Lord's own Apostles are the sources — they who chose nothing of their own invention but who faithfully taught the nations the teaching received from Christ. Even if an angel from heaven were to bring in another gospel, we would consider him accursed.

9.[7] Here is my basic proposition: Christ taught a single clear doctrine which the world must believe. They must seek it so that when they find it, they may believe. Now there can be no endless search when it is a question of a simple, clear doctrine. You must seek until you find and believe when you find it. There is nothing beyond this except to guard what you have believed since part of your belief is precisely that there is nothing further to be believed or sought since you found and believe what was taught. Part of what he taught was the command to seek nothing beyond what he taught. If you still have any doubts, it will be shown that what Christ taught is to be found with us.

13.[8] The Rule of Faith is...that by which we believe: There is but one God who is none other than the Creator of the universe, who made all things out of nothing, through his Word who was sent forth, the first of all things. (We believe) that the Logos, called his Son, in the name of God was variously seen by the Patriarchs, heard by the Prophets, finally sent down by the Spirit and Power of God the Father into the Virgin Mary, became flesh in her womb, was born of her, Jesus Christ. After that, he preached the new Law and the new promise of the Kingdom of Heaven, worked miracles, was crucified, rose on the third day, was taken up into heaven and sits at the right hand of the Father. (We believe) that he sent in his place the power of the Holy Spirit who leads those who believe, that he will come in glory to bring the saints to the enjoyment of eternal life and the heavenly promises and to judge the unbeliever with everlasting fire, and the resurrection and the restoration of the flesh for each group. As shall be demonstrated, this rule was

[7]Text: CCL 1. 195
[8]Text: CCL 1. 197-198

taught by Christ. We have no further questions except those stirred up by heretics. Their very questioning makes more heretics.

14.[9] So long as the content of the rule remains unchanged, you may question, discuss and satisfy your curiosity to your heart's content, if something seems unclear or uncertain. Surely there must be some learned fellow Christian, endowed with knowledge, or someone with greater "sophistication" who, like yourself, feels he must keep seeking. Yet when all is said and done, in my opinion, you would be far better off to remain in your ignorance than to know what you would be far better off not knowing. "Your faith has saved you," (Lk 18.42) Christ said, not your exegetical investigations. The faith has been summed up in the rule; it has its own law and salvation is found in observing that law. Research stems from the desire to know; it glories in its frantic desire to be up-to-date. Let the desire for knowledge give place to faith; let glory give place to salvation. Either let them cease being an obstacle or let them be quiet. To know nothing against the rule is to know everything.

15.[10] Now I come to the point. Up until now I have been directing my argument in a certain direction and setting the stage so that henceforward we may challenge the very basis of our opponents' appeal. They claim to plead on the basis of Scripture and by this manoeuvre immediately sway some people. In the very dispute itself, they wear down the strong, captivate the weak, and send the rest away with a doubt planted in their hearts. Here, then, is where I draw the line: these people are not to be admitted to any discussion of the Scriptures in the first place. If the Scriptures are their strong point, as long as they can get at them, we must look into the question of who properly possess the Scriptures, lest some who have no right be allowed access to them.

16. I have not started off this way because of a lack of confidence or some desire to attack the problem from an unusual angle. Rather this is the primary reason: our faith

[9]Text: CCL 1.198
[10]Text: CCL 1. 199-200

owes a debt of obedience to the Apostle who forbids us to go into certain questions, to open our ears to novel ideas, to meet with a heretic after one admonition (not after one disputation!). He forbade a disputation, indicating rather admonition as the reason for meeting with a heretic. And there is to be only one such occasion because the heretic is not a Christian. And so, he is not to be granted another chance as would be the case with a Christian, before two or three witnesses, since he is being reprimanded precisely for a reason which allows of no discussion with him. Hence a discussion of the Scriptures will be of no use except to upset the stomach or bring on a headache.

20.[11] (Whoever Christ is, or whatever he taught, he taught it plainly and openly.) . . . All this he taught either openly to the people or apart to his disciples, from whom he chose twelve in particular who were to be the teachers of the nations. . . First they went through Judaea bearing witness to their faith in Jesus Christ and founding churches, thence into the whole world, they preached the same teaching of the same faith to the nations. In every city, they founded churches from which other churches have borrowed cuttings from the vine of faith and the seeds of teaching and they continue to borrow them each day that they too may become churches. In this way they too are accounted apostolic, being the sprouts from apostolic churches. Each kind of thing must take its name from its origins. So these churches, numerous and great as they are, are really that single original Church of the Apostles, whence they all come. Thus all are primitive and all are apostolic because they are all one. These are the proofs of unity; they are in peaceful communion with each other; they call each other by the name of brother and sister; they exchange recognized pledges of hospitality. The only law governing them is the unique tradition of the same mystery.

21.[12] (Christ sent preachers with his message.)

How are we to know what they (the Apostles) preached,

---

[11]Text: CCL 1. 201-202
[12]Text: CCL 1. 202-203

i.e. what Christ revealed to them? Here I claim that this is to be resolved only by having recourse to those very churches which the Apostles themselves founded, first by preaching to them in person and afterwards by their letters. If this is correct, then it is obvious that any teaching which is in accord with the teachings of these apostolic churches, these primordial wombs of the faith, is to be counted as the truth, containing as it does without doubt what the churches received from the Apostles, the Apostles from Christ, Christ from God. On the other hand, every teaching must be *a priori* judged as false which gives even a hint of being contrary to the truth of the churches, the Apostles, Christ and God ... We are in communion with the apostolic churches because there is no discrepancy in teaching: this is the testimony of the truth.

25.[13] But, as we have said, it is just as crazy to grant that the Apostles knew all there was to know, that there were no differences in their preaching, yet they were not willing to reveal all the teaching to all the people. Some things they revealed openly to all, but others secretly only to a few and all this because Paul said to Timothy: "O Timothy, guard the deposit." And again: "Keep the good deposit." (1 Tm 6.20) What is this deposit? A secret one so that it should be considered someone else's teaching? ... The context makes it clear that there is nothing about a hidden teaching here; the point is rather that nothing else is to be accepted beyond what he had heard from him and, I suppose, "before many witnesses." If you are not willing to see the Church in these "many witnesses," it is not vital; what is obvious is that what has been put forward in front of "many witnesses" is not a secret teaching.

26.[14] Those who refused to keep silent in synagogues or in public places preached even more freely in church. They could hardly have converted Jews or attracted pagans unless they set out what it was they wanted to be accepted in faith. Nor would they have withheld something from the

[13]Text: CCL 1. 206-207
[14]Text: CCL 1. 208

believing assemblies so that they could secretly entrust it to a few. Although they may have discussed certain matters with an inner circle, so to speak, it is not credible that they introduced another rule of faith, one different from, and contrary to, what the Catholic Church proclaimed for all, so that they spoke of one God in the assembly and another at home; one type of Christ in public, another in secret; one hope of resurrection for the many, another for the few, when at the very same time in other letters they were begging that all say the same thing and that there be no schisms and dissensions in the Church, because all preached the same message, whether it be Paul or the others.

28.[15] Let us suppose that all have been in error, that even the Apostle was deceived about what he was to preach. Imagine that the Holy Spirit had taken no particular interest in bringing any to the truth although Christ had sent him for that purpose and the Father had asked him to be the teacher of the truth. And that God's overseer, Christ's vicar, neglected his duty, permitting the churches for a while to understand and believe something other than what the Apostles had preached. Is it at all likely that so many churches would have stumbled into one and the same faith? Among so many it is impossible that they all would have ended at the same spot. If the churches had gone astray, their teaching would certainly be divergent. On the other hand, where unity is found among many, we are dealing not with error but with tradition. Will anyone dare to assert that error lay at the origins of the tradition?

32.[16] (Will they claim that their heresies go back to apostolic times?)

Otherwise, if any claim to plant themselves in the age of the Apostles in order to make it seem that their ideas were handed down by the Apostles because they existed under the Apostles, we can say: Let them show the origins of their churches, let them unroll the list of their bishops, (showing) through a succession coming from the very beginning, that

[15]Text: CCL 1. 209
[16]Text: CCL 1. 212-213

their first bishop had as his authority and predecessor someone from among the number of the Apostles or apostolic men and, further, that he did not stray from the Apostles. In this way the apostolic churches present their earliest records. The church of Smyrna, for example, records that Polycarp was named by John; the Romans, that Clement was ordained by Peter. In just the same way, the other churches show who were made bishops by the Apostles and who transmitted the apostolic seed to them.

Let the heretics try to invent something like that. But after their blasphemy, nothing is beyond them. Even if they can come up with something, it will do them no good. Their very teaching, when compared with that of the Apostles, from its diversity and internal contradictions, will show itself for what it is — that it has no Apostle or apostolic man at its origins because just as the Apostles did not contradict each other in their teachings, so the next generation taught nothing contrary to what the Apostles had preached, unless, of course, you believe they preached something different from what they had learned from the Apostles. This is the test which can be demanded by those churches which cannot historically claim as founder either an Apostle or an apostolic man because they came much later. New churches are still being founded every day. Since they are in agreement on the faith, they are to be considered no less apostolic because of their kinship in doctrine. Thus let all the heresies challenged by our churches to furnish this two-fold proof show for what reasons they consider themselves apostolic. But in fact they are not apostolic. They are not received into peace and communion by churches that are in any way really apostolic, principally because they cannot be apostolic, given the variations in their teachings.

36.[17] Well now, you can make better use of your curiosity for your own salvation, you know. Have a look at the apostolic churches, those places where the thrones of the Apostles even now preside in their places, where their authentic letters are still read, bringing back to us how they

[17]Text: CCL 1. 216-217

sounded and the way they looked. If Achaea is close by, you have Corinth. If you are not far from Macedonia, you have Philippi. If you can go to Asia, there is Ephesus. If you are in the vicinity of Italy, you have Rome, which is also our closest apostolic see.

Blessed is that church upon which the Apostles poured out their entire teaching along with their blood. This is where Peter suffered like his Lord; where Paul was crowned with John (the Baptist's) death and where John the Apostle later, cast into boiling oil but suffering no ill effects, was exiled to an island. Let us see what she learned and what she taught. With the same seal as the African church, she has known one God and Lord, Creator of the universe, and Jesus Christ, (born) of the Virgin Mary, the Son of the Creator God, and the resurrection of the flesh. She joins the Law and the Prophets with the Gospels and the apostolic letters, thence she draws the faith. This faith she seals with water, clothes with the Holy Spirit, feeds with the Eucharist, exhorts to martyrdom, and accepts no one contrary to this teaching. This is the teaching, I won't say that predicted the heresies to come, but rather out of which the heresies came. But they are no longer of it, from the time they came to be against it.

37.[18] If this is the way things are: the truth is judged to belong to us, i.e., "to those who walk according to this rule" (Gal 6.16) which the churches received from the Apostles, the Apostles from Christ, Christ from God. It is clear that our initial proposition is established: that heretics are not to be allowed to enter a plea on the basis of the Scriptures, because we, without having to resort to the Scriptures, have demonstrated that the Scriptures do not belong to them. If they are heretics, they cannot be Christians... Not being Christians, they have no right to the Christian writings. We, on the other hand, have every right to say to them: who are you? Where did you come from and when did you arrive? What are you doing on my property since you are not my people? By what right, Marcion, do you cut down my trees?

[18]Text: CCL I. 217-218

By whose permission, Valentinus, are you diverting my streams? By whose authority, Apelles, are you moving my boundary markers? I own this. As for the rest of you, why do you think you have the right to sow and graze here? I own it; I have owned it for a long time; I owned it before you came along. I have authentic documents from the very ones who were the original owners. I am the heir of the Apostles. As they stipulated in their will, as they bequeathed in trust and confirmed by an oath, just so do I keep faith with them. But you they have always disinherited and disowned as strangers and enemies. Why are heretics strangers to and enemies of the Apostles except for their different teachings which each has brought forward or at least accepted, putting his own will ahead of the Apostles.

38.[19] Wherever you find diversity of teaching, this is to be attributed to falsification of the Scriptures or of their interpretation. Those who wished to have a different teaching were of necessity forced to alter the material sources of the teaching. They could not have a different doctrine unless they first had different sources. Just as for them, there could be no corruption of doctrine without first corrupting the sources, so for us, there can be no integrity of doctrine unless we guard the integrity of doctrine's sources. What is there in our sources that is contrary to our doctrine? Have we brought in something of our own invention, something glaringly contradicted by Scripture, so that we must try to cover it up by adding or dropping something or by changing something? What we are, this is what the Scriptures have been from their very beginning. We are of them and always have been before anyone tried to change them. Every change obviously comes after the original. It stems from jealousy and there can be no jealousy before there is some original to be jealous of...

41.[20] I don't want to end without sketching the heretical life-style, how pointless, how worldly and merely human it is. There is no seriousness, no authority, no discipline — it

[19]Text: CCL 1. 218
[20]Text: CCL 1. 221-223

all fits right in with their faith! First of all, you are never sure who is a catechumen and who is already baptized. They are all there; they all hear and pray together. If some pagan should drop by, they will cast what is holy to the dogs and cast pearls (counterfeits!) before swine. The subverting of discipline they prefer to call simplicity; concern about discipline they call affectation. They are for intercommunion all around. Exegetical divergencies are no problem for them provided they agree in attacking the truth. They are all proud; they all promise knowledge. Their catechumens are baptized before they have received instruction. Their women are irrepressible. They have no scruples about teaching, debating, conducting exorcisms, promising cures, perhaps even baptizing. They ordain hastily with little forethought or investigation. They don't last very long. Sometimes they take the newly baptized, sometimes men too closely bound to the secular world, sometimes even people who have abandoned our Church, perhaps hoping that honors will bind them in a way the truth could not. Nowhere is it easier to gain advancement than in the rebel camp: just being there is reason for promotion. And so, one person is the bishop today; someone else tomorrow. Today's deacon is tomorrow's reader; a priest one day becomes a layman the next. For they impose priestly duties even on the laity.

42. Concerning the ministry of the word, what shall I say? Their real interest is not to convert pagans but to pervert Christians. They get a much bigger thrill out of ruining those who are all right than out of righting those who were ruined. Since their own work consists primarily not in building anything of their own but in the destruction of the truth, they first undermine our own works to build their own. Deprive them of their problems with the Law of Moses and the prophets and the Creator God and they fall silent. So it is that their real work is the demolition of standing buildings rather than the restoration of fallen ruins. These are the only purposes for which they show themselves humble, agreeable and modest. For the rest they never even respect their own leaders. This is the reason why heretics rarely suffer schism,

or when they have them, they are difficult to perceive: viz., their opposition to us is the only thing that holds them together. I do not think I am lying when I assert that they not only differ among themselves in their teachings since each one fashions his doctrines as he likes but they also differ from their own founders who themselves shaped their teachings to suit themselves. Try as it may, a thing's later stages cannot shake off its nature or its original heritage... In fine, when you take a close look at any heresy, you will find that on many points they no longer agree with their founder. Most of them simply have no churches; they wander off without mother, without home, bereft of faith...

43. Well known also are the dealings of heretics with quacks, astrologers, philosophers, any one dedicated to the "SEARCH FOR TRUTH!" They never stop repeating "Seek and you will find." The worth of their faith can be estimated from their lifestyle. Strictness of discipline is the best measure of the truth of any doctrine. They deny that God should be feared: thus for them everything is free and easy. Where is God not feared except where he is not found? Where God is not found, neither is there any truth; and where there is no truth, needless to say, you can guess what kind of discipline there will be. But when God is present, there will also be found the fear of God which is the beginning of wisdom. Where the fear of God is found, there will also be found: decent seriousness, unsleeping zeal, concerned care, thoughtful choice, carefully considered communion, preferment only when deserved, religious submission, devoted service, a modest advance, a Church united, and all things godly.

AGAINST MARCION

IV.5[21] In fine, if it is a fact that what is earlier has a greater claim to be the truth, and that that which comes from the beginning is necessarily the earlier, what was from the

[21]Text: CCL 1. 550-552

beginning comes from the Apostles. So it will be agreed that what has been held most sacred in the churches founded by the Apostles is that which has been handed down from the Apostles themselves. Let us see what milk the Corinthians were given to drink by Paul, to what rule the Galatians were recalled, what the Philippians, Thessalonians and Ephesians read, what the Romans who are nearest (of all these) to us have to say, they to whom Peter and Paul bequeathed their Gospel signed in their own blood. We also have churches founded by John; for although Marcion repudiates the Apocalypse, the list of their bishops, traced backwards will be found to have John at the beginning. Just so is the pedigree of all the others known.

Thus I say among them — not just those founded by Apostles but among all those united in the communion of the mysteries, that the Gospel of Luke has existed since its first appearance, whereas Marcion's Gospel is unknown to most, but those who know it, condemn it. He has his own churches, of course, late offspring of a spiritual infidelity. If you check their pedigree, you will find it much more apostate than apostolic since Marcion or one of his crowd founded it. Marcionites make churches as wasps make combs. The same authority of the apostolic churches will support the other gospels as well. . . (The other gospels have at least as much claim to authority as Luke's which Marcion singled out.)

. . . We use this type of summary argument when we defend the Gospel faith against heretics, using the temporal prescription argument against the late-coming counterfeits, and the authority of the churches which protects the tradition of the Apostles; because the truth of necessity comes before falsity and it comes from those by whom it was handed down.

THE SOLDIER'S CROWN; THE VEILING OF VIRGINS

In two works, *The Soldier's Crown* and *The Veiling of Virgins*, Tertullian discusses traditions. In the first, he tells of a Christian soldier who refused to wear a crown of leaves to receive a bonus from the emperor on the grounds that it was a practice involving pagan worship. He suffered for his conviction. Tertullian used the incident to comment on the question of Christian practices not found in Scripture. As always happened when the Fathers discussed such "traditions," they spoke almost exclusively of liturgical practices. How, asked Tertullian, do Christians justify such traditional practices, if they demand scriptural proof for everything (such as the prohibition against wearing crowns!)?

As we have seen before, Tertullian, the master controversialist, can argue as it suits him. As a rigorist, he wished all women to be veiled. In his native Carthage, young, unmarried women, including dedicated Christian virgins, were not. Here he argues against the custom of his own area, invoking the customs of other churches. In this treatise, he cites the rule of faith once again.

The Soldier's Crown

2.[22] I would say that no Christian wears a crown except in time of trial. All observe this custom from catechumens to confessors and martyrs, even apostates. I want you to see where this custom we are discussing comes from... It is very easy to demand chapter and verse in Scripture. Where precisely is there a prohibition against wearing a crown? I say: Show me where it says a Christian *may* wear a crown. When people demand scriptural proof for something they reject, they admit by that fact that their own opinion should be able to appeal to scriptural proof. For if it is claimed that we may wear a crown because Scripture does not forbid it, I will come back immediately with this: We may not wear a crown because Scripture does not command it. What should the practice be? Accept both, as if neither is prohibited, or reject both as if neither is commanded? "But what is not forbidden is permitted." Rather, I say, that is forbidden which is not clearly permitted.

3. How long must we go at each other like this? In fact, we have an ancient practice which by its very existence presents

[22]Text: CCL 2. 1041-1044

the solution. For if no scriptural passage has settled this, custom has strengthened the practice, a custom which beyond any doubt flows from tradition. How can something be the custom if it has not been handed down? But, you will object, even when pleading tradition, a scriptural source must be shown. Let us ask, then, whether a tradition must be received if there is no written source. Clearly, we shall say 'no' if we can find no other examples of customs without a clear scriptural source, whose sole claim is tradition yet have gained the force of custom.

To begin with Baptism: when we are about to enter the water, but a little before, under the bishop's hand, in the midst of the assembly, we solemnly declare that we renounce the devil and his pomp and his angels. After that we are immersed three times, answering somewhat more fully than the Lord required in the Gospel. Right after that, we taste a mixture of milk and honey and from that day for a week we keep from our daily bath. The sacrament of the Eucharist, which the Lord entrusted to all and at a meal, we receive at pre-dawn services, and from no other hand than that of those who preside. We celebrate annually the sacrifice for the deceased on their birthdays. We consider it wrong to fast on Sundays or to worship on our knees that day. It is the same practice during the period of rejoicing from Easter to Pentecost. We are very careful not to allow anything from the cup or the bread to fall to the ground. We make the sign of the cross on our foreheads at every turn, coming and going, dressing, putting on our shoes, waking, eating, lighting the lamps, going to bed, sitting down, in all other actions of our daily life.

4. For these and many other parts of the Christian life and practices, if you seek one, you will find no scriptural command. Rather tradition will be brought forward as the origin, with custom to confirm and faith to require its continued observance. You yourself will come to see, or someone who has realized it will teach you, that reason supports tradition, custom and faith. In the meantime, you can safely presume that there is a reason why the custom should be observed...

If I cannot find a law, it follows that tradition has given the practice the force of custom and would receive at a future time the support of Paul, from an interpretation of reason. From these examples, you will admit that a tradition even though without specific scriptural foundation, because it is observed, can be defended, when it is confirmed by custom, which is itself a suitable witness from the very length of its observance that a tradition has been tested and approved. In civil affairs, custom can have the force of law when a law is lacking and it makes no difference whether there is a basis in something written or in reason only so long as reason supports the law. Moreover, if law is based on reason, then anything based on reason will be a law, wherever it comes from. Or do you not believe that it is permitted to anyone of the faithful to conceive and to establish (a practice) so long as it is fitting to God, promotes discipline, and is profitable for salvation...?

The Veiling of Virgins

1.[23] (Virgins should be veiled from a certain age.)

The truth demands this and there can be no prescriptive argument against it, neither on the basis of the passage of time, nor because certain persons have supported the contrary custom, nor on the basis that certain regions have a privilege to be different. These latter are the factors that give rise to custom, at the beginning arising out of ignorance or simplicity. Custom is strengthened by observance over time and thus is given a claim against truth. But our Lord Jesus Christ called himself the truth, not the custom. If Christ is eternal and before all things, equally then truth of old is eternal. Let those look to themselves for whom that is new which is simply old in itself. Heresies are exposed less by their novelty than by the truth. Whatever smacks of being against the truth, this will be heresy, even if it involve a custom of long standing. It is your own shortcoming if you do not know something. If little is known about something,

[23]Text: CCL 2. 1209-1211

there is at least as great an obligation to look into it as there is an obligation to acknowledge what is commonly accepted.

The one and only unchanging and unchangeable thing is the rule of faith which says that we must believe in one God Almighty, the Creator of the universe, and his Son, Jesus Christ, born of the Virgin Mary. He was crucified under Pontius Pilate, raised from the dead on the third day, received into the heavens, and sits now at the right hand of the Father. He will come to judge the living and the dead through the resurrection of the flesh. This law of faith remains unchanged but all other matters involving discipline and life-style allow the "novelty" of reform, knowing that the grace of God is active and making progress up to the very end. Why should anyone think that, while the Devil is always at work and daily comes up with new inspirations for evil, the activity of God would have stopped altogether or ceased to advance? The Lord sent the Paraclete so that, inasmuch as human weakness was not able to grasp everything at the beginning, nevertheless, little by little, discipline might be directed, ordered and brought to perfection by that vicar of the Lord, the Holy Spirit. (Jn 16. 12-15)... What is the Paraclete doing day after day unless it be this: the promotion of discipline, the revealing of the Scriptures, the reformation of our understanding, in general, progress for the better? Nothing is accomplished without the passage of time and each thing awaits its proper time... (Nature grows and develops.)... So it is with Righteousness — for the God of Righteousness and of creation is one and the same. It was first in an elementary state, fearing God by nature, thence through the Law and the prophets to infancy, bursting into the fervor of youth with the Gospel and now coming to maturity with the Paraclete. He must be, after Christ, the only one to be called and honored as Master. He does not speak of himself but what Christ commanded him to say. He is the only guide because the only one after Christ. Those who have accepted him, value the truth above custom...

2. (Right customs observed in other local churches.)

For the present I do not wish to regard this custom as the truth. Let it stand as just a custom for the time being that I may compare one custom with another. Throughout Greece and several adjacent areas, many of the churches veil their virgins. This is done even in some places in our corner of the world so that no one can blame this custom solely on the Greeks and other foreigners. But I have brought up the Eastern churches because they had as founders Apostles or apostolic men and others I shall not name now. These churches have the same authority for their customs. They put forward their antiquity and their founders with greater effect than those founded later. Which shall we observe? Which shall we choose? We cannot repudiate a custom which we are unable to condemn insofar as it is not foreign to us. We cannot label "foreign" those with whom we share the right to communion and the name of "brother." They and we have one faith, one God, the same Christ, the same hope, the same baptismal mysteries, in short, we are one Church. Whatever belongs to our people belongs to us. Otherwise, you are dividing the Body.

As in any case where there is diversity, doubt or uncertainty, you must investigate to see which of the two customs better befits the discipline God wants. Obviously, the one to choose is the one that leaves virgins unknown but to God...

> As Tertullian became more closely identified with Montanism, his Catholic opponents were happy to make use of arguments he himself had earlier formulated on the priority of orthodoxy and the evil of novelty. Were not the new, rigoristic practices advocated by the later Tertullian automatically suspect? Was it the Holy Spirit or the evil spirit who suggested such changes? Tertullian grants the novelty but argues 1) that the rule of faith (the teaching on God and Christ) has not been altered in the slightest, and 2) Satan would never advocate stricter discipline.

MONOGAMY

2.[24] At this point we must stop and ask: Do we find the Paraclete teaching something that should be considered either a novelty over against Catholic tradition or something burdensome compared to the lighter burden (of the Lord)? On both of these issues, the Lord himself has spoken when he said: "I have much more to tell you but you cannot bear it now. When the Holy Spirit comes, however, he will guide you into all truth." (Jn 16.12-13) He thus indicates that he will teach things that can be considered novelties, since they were not put forward previously and somewhat burdensome — the very reason why they were not announced earlier. Therefore, you say, by this sort of argument anything new and burdensome can be attributed to the Paraclete. Not at all. For our spiritual enemy would make himself all too obvious by the contradictions in his teaching, first of all by perverting the rule of faith and after that, perverting orderly discipline. Because he must try to corrupt first of all that which is more important, i.e., the faith first since this comes before discipline. A person must first be heretical in his teaching about God and then only concerning his law. But the Paraclete, having many things to teach which the Lord, according to his plan, put off until he should come, will first bear witness to Christ himself such as we already believe him to be, and will glorify him along with the whole work of God the Creator, and will remind us about him. Basing himself on the fundamental beliefs of the rule of faith, he will then reveal many of those things which pertain to discipline, the purity of the teaching serving as a guarantee for them...

ON PURITY

In his treatise on *Purity*, one of his last works from his Montanist period, Tertullian takes a hard line on the forgiveness of Christians who committed serious sins after their baptism. Here it is the spiritual who have the

[24]Text: CCL 2. 1230

power to forgive sins; those who hold Church office, as such, do not have such authority.

21.[25] Show me, then, apostolic man, examples of your prophecies so that I may recognize their divine origin and prove that you have the power to forgive sins. But if, on the other hand, the office you hold finds its raison d'être in the supervision of discipline and you are to preside as a servant rather than as a tyrant, who do you think you are, or how great, that you forgive sins? Since you are neither prophet nor Apostle, you simply do not possess the power to forgive. "Yet," you will protest, "the Church has the power to forgive sins." I grant this and I am more careful about it as well for I possess the word of the Paraclete who spoke through the new prophets: "The Church can forgive sins, but I will not do it, lest worse things result." What if some false spirit of prophecy made this statement? The Devil would have commended himself by his leniency and eased others onto the road to crime. Or if here too he sought to imitate the Spirit of Truth, therefore the Spirit of Truth can indeed extend mercy to fornicators but is not willing to do so because greater harm will come to more people...

What has this to do with your Church, O Catholic? This power is given to Peter personally and then to spiritual men, to an Apostle or a prophet. For the Church itself is properly, and in principle, the Spirit himself, in whom there is the Trinity of one Divinity, the Father, the Son and the Holy Spirit. The Spirit brings together that Church which the Lord said is found where three are gathered. Henceforward, any member of those who accept this faith is reckoned a church by the one who founded and consecrated it. And so the Church will indeed forgive sins but this Church is the Church of the Spirit, acting through a man of the Spirit, not the Church equated with a group of bishops. For the right of decision belongs to the Master, not the servant, to God, not the bishop.

[25]Text: CCL 2. 1326-1328

FASTING

In his work of *Fasting*, we have one of the earliest references to councils.

13.[26] In addition, throughout the Greek areas in various places, councils consisting of representatives from all the churches are held. Here they discuss together the most important' questions. It is a sort of manifestation of the whole Church, one that commands great respect.

[26]Text: CCL 2. 1272

Chapter Four

OTHER THIRD CENTURY DEVELOPMENTS

Hippolytus of Rome

Hippolytus (c.170-c.236), though a theologian of Rome, still wrote in Greek. He apparently was a noteworthy preacher and writer. Early in the third century he became so embroiled in controversy with bishop Callistus (+ c.222) that he became the first anti-Pope or schismatic bishop of Rome in history. He led a small community which claimed to preserve the rigor of the ancient discipline of the Church. According to tradition, he died reconciled to the Church and is honored as a martyr.

THE REFUTATION OF ALL HERESIES

1.Preface[1] We will offer men no small assistance for the conduct of their lives, to keep them from going astray, i.e., that all may see clearly these hidden and unseen mysteries which the others, holding back, reveal only to the initiated. But no one can refute them save the Holy Spirit handed down in the Church. The Apostles were the first to receive

[1]Text: GCS 26. 2-3

him and they communicated the Spirit to those who believed rightly. We are their successors, sharing in the same grace of high-priesthood and of teaching. As guardians of the Church, we do not grow drowsy nor do we keep silent about right teaching. We do not grow weary of working with all our strength of soul and body trying to give meritorious service in return for God's good gifts... We shall not restrict ourselves to bringing to light errors to refute them but we shall also proclaim whatever the truth has received from the Father of grace and put at the service of men... It is not by drawing on the Holy Scriptures nor by guarding the tradition of some holy person that the heretics have formulated these doctrines. They have rushed headlong into them but their beliefs find their inspiration in the wisdom of the Greeks.

THE APOSTOLIC TRADITION

Preface[2] Now moved "by your love for all the saints" (Eph 1.15), we have come to the most important part of the tradition proper to the churches so that those who have been well taught will keep the tradition which has lasted until now. If they study the exposition which we have made, they will remain firmly set... The Holy Spirit confers on those who believe correctly a fullness of grace so that they will know how those who preside in the Church ought to teach and guard all things.

PSEUDO-HIPPOLYTUS AGAINST ARTEMON (IN EUSEBIUS, CHURCH HISTORY)

V.28.3-4,6[3] These people claim that all the men of earlier times and the Apostles themselves received and taught these things which they now preach and that the truth of the proclamation was preserved until the time of Victor, who was the thirteenth bishop in Rome after Peter. From the

[2]Text: SC 11 bis. 38,40
[3]Text: SC 41. 75

time of his successor, Zephyrinus, the truth was changed. What they are saying might have some plausibility if, first of all, the divine Scriptures were not against them. How then, with the Church's mind having been made clear for so many years, are we to believe that Christians up until the time of Victor preached in the way these people claim?

Alexandria: A Different Tradition Clement and Origen

The early theologians of Alexandria, one of the great cities of the ancient world and an intellectual center for Jews and Greeks alike, are in many ways in a class by themselves. Clement (+ c.215) was for a while the leader of a school in the city and is traditionally considered the teacher of Origen (c.185-c.253), one of the greatest of patristic theologians. Among the characteristics of their theological approach may be cited a greater openness to the contribution of pagan culture and philosophy and a pronounced tendency toward the allegorical or figurative interpretation of the Scriptures. In contrast to the Latin African theologians, they rarely comment directly on the organizational aspects of the Church. Clement in particular speaks in terms reminiscent of Gnosticism. For him, the Christian Gnostic, a combination of sanctity, mysticism, intellectual acumen and learning, is the true holy person, the saint. Clement also speaks in terms of a succession but this succession is also reminiscent of Gnosticism because it is a succession of teachers (like himself) more than a succession of bishops. Here the *didaskaloi*, the teachers, are a more important authority factor in Church teaching than you would gather is the case anywhere else in the Church from the reading of other patristic texts.

STROMATA

I.11[4] (Speaking of his own teachers, Clement writes:)
But they, safeguarding the true tradition of the blessed
teaching which comes straight from the Apostles Peter,
James, John and Paul and transmitted from father to son
(though few sons are comparable to their fathers) have come
down to us with the help of God to deposit in us those
ancestral and apostolic seeds. I.12. And I know very well
that they will rejoice, not especially because of this present
work, but solely because that which was deposited has been
preserved. And I think thoughts such as these are thoughts
of a soul that longs to keep the blessed tradition intact. "He
who loves wisdom makes his Father glad." (Prv 29.3)

I.55[5] Since the tradition is not common or public at least
for the one who is fully aware of the greatness of the teaching, therefore it is right to hide the "wisdom" expressed "in
mystery" which the Son of God taught. The prophet Isaiah
had his tongue purified by fire that he might be able to
describe his vision. It is not only our tongue but our ears
which must be purified, if we are going to try to be partakers
of the truth. Previously such thoughts kept me from writing
and even now I am careful not "to cast pearls before swine"
for fear that "they will trample them under foot and perhaps
even tear you to shreds" as the Lord declares. (Mt 7.6)

VI.61[6] If then we say that Christ himself is Wisdom and
that it is his power which worked through the prophets and
which still instructs us through the Gnostic tradition just as
he himself taught the holy Apostles in the time of his
(earthly) presence, then Wisdom is the Gnosis, which is
knowledge as well as a valid and sure comprehension of the
things that are, will be, and have been, as they have been
revealed and made known by the Son of God. And if the
goal of the wise man is contemplation, the one who is still
only a philosopher may aspire to divine knowledge but does

[4]Text: SC 30. 52
[5]Text: SC 30. 89
[6]Text: GCS 52 (15). 462

not yet attain it so long as he has not received the instruction which explains to him the prophetic utterance through which he may learn about how things of the present, past and future, are, have been and will be. This very Gnosis has come down through a series of successions in unwritten form from the Apostles to a few...

VI. 124[7] The liars then in reality are...those who err in essentials and reject the Lord...Those who do not cite or transmit the Scriptures in a manner worthy of God and the Lord. The understanding and the discipline of the holy tradition according to the teaching of the Lord as received from his Apostles is a deposit for which we are responsible to God. "What you hear in private" i.e., in a hidden sense and in mystery (for these things are said figuratively to be 'spoken in private'), "Proclaim it from the housetops." (Mt 10.27) Receive the Scriptures with minds raised on high, pass them on, appreciating their sublimity and explain the Scriptures according to the rule of truth.

VI.125 The Apostles accordingly say of the Lord that "All these lessons Jesus taught the crowds in the form of parables. He spoke to them in parables only." (Mt 13.34) and if "through him all things came into being and apart from him nothing came to be." (Jn 1.3) consequently, prophecy and the Law also came through him and were taught by him in parables. "All things are plain...and right to those who attain knowledge." (Prv 8.9), says Scripture, that is, to those who receive and hold to the interpretation of the Scriptures according to the rule of the Church, such as they have been revealed by him. The rule of the Church teaches the agreement and harmony of the Law and the Prophets with the Covenant given in the time of the Lord's presence among us.

VII.103[8] And if those also who follow heresies venture to avail themselves of the prophets, first it should be noted, they do not make use of all the Scriptures...but, selecting ambiguous expressions, they twist them to their own opin-

[7]Text: GCS 52 (15). 494-495
[8]Text: GCS 17^2. 73

ions...not looking to the meaning but just manipulating words.

VII.104 For us, the Gnostic alone, having grown old in the Scriptures, preserving the Apostolic and ecclesiastical correctness of doctrine, living a life strictly according to the Gospel, is led by the Lord to discover the proofs from the Law and the prophets which he seeks. For the life of the Gnostic, in my view, is nothing other than a life of living and teaching in accordance with the tradition of the Lord.

ORIGEN

Clement's student and successor as head of the Alexandrian school was Origen. He is considered by some to be the greatest theologian among the Fathers. In a time when originality of thought was not always appreciated, Origen's was an original and searching intellect. His penchant for bold hypotheses did not endear him to some in the Church. Even while still a layman and very young, he came to attract attention and became something of a theological oracle in the East. He travelled widely but after his ordination as a presbyter in Palestine, around the year 230, he had to transfer the location of his teaching and writing activities from Alexandria to Caesarea in Palestine. Here he suffered imprisonment and torture during the persecution of Decius (250), dying a few years later. During his lifetime, and even more so after, his ideas, real or alleged, made him a center of controversy. Similar in many ways to Clement, he is less esoteric and often expressed the desire to be nothing greater than "a man of the Church."

The treatise *On First Principles* (*De principiis*; *Peri Archōn*) is Origen's best known and most controversial work. It is a work of his youth. The Scriptures contain something for everyone, in Origen's view, something of profit for the simple believer as well as for the person able to probe deeply into mysteries and hidden meanings. The Holy Spirit was thoughtful enough to provide intellectual challenges for future theologians such as Origen.

On First Principles

1. Preface[9] Many of those who profess to believe in Christ are not in agreement, not only on points of small or minimal significance, but even on questions of great or very great importance, i.e., concerning God or the Lord Jesus Christ himself or the Holy Spirit and not only on these questions, but also on the subject of his creatures such as the Dominations or the holy Powers. For all these reasons, it seems necessary to start by laying down a definite line on each of these things and a clear rule and then to proceed from there to ask questions about other matters. Many Greeks and barbarians have promised the truth but, starting from the moment when we came to believe that Christ is the Son of God, we recognized that their ideas were only false opinions. Similarly there are many who think they are Christian believers, yet many of these same people in fact believe differently from those who went before them. The Church's preaching has been handed down through an orderly succession from the Apostles and remains in the Church until the present. That alone is to be believed as the truth which in no way departs from ecclesiastical and apostolic tradition.

3. However, you must know that the holy Apostles, preaching the faith of Christ, have transmitted with complete openness those teachings which they believed indispensable for all the faithful, even for those who seemed to be quite incapable of searching into divine knowledge. But they left the explanation of their teachings to be investigated by those who should deserve the excelling gifts of the Spirit and who received through the Holy Spirit the particular graces of the word, wisdom and knowledge. On other matters, they simply declared that these things were so without explaining the why and the wherefore, doubtless in order that the most studious of those who came after them might become lovers of wisdom — I refer to those who would work to be worthy and capable of receiving wisdom — and might be able to find an opportunity to show forth the results of their genius.

[9]Text: SC 252. 78-80, 84-86, 88

7. Here is another point of the Church's preaching: this world was created and began to exist at a certain point and will come to an end because of its corruptible nature. But questions such as: "What existed before the world?"; "What will come after it?" have no obvious answers because there is no clear teaching on this in the preaching of the Church. Another point: the Scriptures have been written by the Spirit of God and they have not only a surface meaning but there is also another meaning hidden from the majority of people. For in reality, the things that are written down are just figures of certain mysteries and the images of divine things. On this the entire Church is of one mind: the whole Law is spiritual but the spiritual content is not known to all but only to those to whom the grace of the Holy Spirit in the word of Wisdom and knowledge is given...

10. Here, then, are all the basic elements that can be used if someone, taking all the points into account, should wish to put together an orderly body of teaching according to the commandment: "Light for yourselves the light of knowledge." (Hos 10.12 LXX) Making use of clear and compelling arguments, he will examine what is true in each individual point and, as we said, will construct a single body (of doctrine), by taking examples and affirmations from the things he finds in the Holy Scriptures or which he shall find as conclusions validly drawn from Scripture by logical deductions.

A Fragment from the Commentary on 1 Corinthians

Fragment 19[10] But let us look at this: "May you learn from us not to go beyond what is set down..." (1 Cor 4.6). If someone who is a spiritual novice wishes, before he has fulfilled what is written, to rise beyond what is written, he will simply demonstrate that he does not even understand what is written... The preachers of heresies claim that they have traditions and assert that they go beyond what is written; for our Saviour gave these traditions to his disciples

[10]Text: *Journal of Theological Studies* 9 (1908) 357

secretly and the Apostles in turn gave them to this one or that. And by such tales, "they deceived the simpleminded." (Rom 16.18)

Commentary on the Letter to the Romans

X.11[11] Do you hear the Apostle when he says: "I have written to you...in parts (of this letter)." (Rom 15.15)? I believe that although even Paul himself claims to know only in part, he in fact knew more, indeed a great deal more than he wrote down. Like someone who knows many things, yet does not dare to reveal many of them, he claims that he is being very bold in committing anything at all to writing. But when he says: "...by way of reminder. (I take this liberty because God) has given me the grace." (Rom 15.15), he indicates that he has already spoken of such matters and indeed has often discussed the mysteries. But since those things which are merely spoken of are easily forgotten, he says that by means of those few things which I have written to you by the grace given to me, I am reminding you of the things which I earlier discussed with you at greater length.

A Homily on the Book of Numbers

> Origen rarely discusses issues of Church government, but when he does, his comments often speak of corruption in the Church. Here he laments irregularities in the elections of bishops.

9.1[12] They (the just) should be exalted (by comparison to their inferiors) at the same time in order to give an example to future generations, so that no one will be so arrogant and presumptuous to take the episcopal dignity without having received it from God. He should yield to the man who has not been urged on by human ambition, nor corrupt politics, who has not usurped it by a few well-placed "donations," but who got where he is only by a recognition of his own merits and by the will of God.

[11]Text: PG 14. 1267-1268
[12]Text: GCS 30. 56

22.4[13] Let us admire the greatness of Moses. As he was about to depart from this life, he prayed God to choose a leader for his people. What are you doing, Moses? Don't you have sons of your own, Gershom and Eliezer? If you lack confidence in them, what about your brother, a great man? Why don't you ask God to make them the leaders of the people?

Would that the princes of the Church, instead of designating in their wills those linked to them by ties of blood or family relationships and instead of trying to set up dynasties in the Church, might learn to rely on God's judgment and far from choosing as human feelings urge, would leave the designations of their successors entirely in God's hands. Could not Moses have chosen a leader for the people and chosen him by a wise judgment, a right and just decision...? Who could have chosen a leader more wisely than Moses? But he did not do so. He made no such choice. He did not dare.

Why not? In order to avoid giving those who came after him an example of presumption. Listen: "May the Lord, the God of the spirits of all mankind, set over the community a man who shall act as their leader in all things, to guide them in all their actions..." (Nm 27.16-17) If a great man like Moses did not take upon himself the choice of a leader for the people, the election of his successor, who then will dare, among this people which gives its vote under the influence of emotion, or perhaps of money; who will dare then, even in the ranks of the priests, judge himself capable of pronouncing on this, unless by means of a revelation obtained through prayers and supplications addressed to the Lord?

Episcopal Authority: Cyprian of Carthage

Cyprian was bishop of Carthage from 248-258. Hardly had he become bishop when a serious persecution broke

[13]Text: GCS 30. 208

out under the emperor Decius, a persecution which seriously shook his community. Large numbers of Christians defected; some without even the appearance of resistance, some with a certain eagerness. When the trial was over, many of these same people sought to return to the Church. Cyprian tried to pursue a middle path between two extremes. The case of each person was to be examined and a penance befitting his/her sin determined. But extremists at each end of the spectrum did not want to accept this moderate solution. Cyprian, faced with the threat of schism, elaborated a theology of the unity of the local church.

The local church of Rome faced a similar crisis. Cyprian and his Roman counterpart worked closely together. Cyprian's theology of the Church spoke of the unity of the bishops among themselves, yet his often reiterated view was that each bishop was responsible to God alone, thus fostering a type of episcopalism.

Cyprian also frequently made use of the image of the *cathedra Petri* or "chair of Peter" in works such as the treatise *On the Unity of the Church*. Historically, there has been much ink spilled over the two versions of the fourth chapter of this work. One version is seen as the "Petrine" version, pointing to Rome as the chair of Peter and the principal authority in the Church. The other version, the one given here, stresses unity. Most recent scholarship views Cyprian as the author of *both* versions. Moreover, both versions mirror this "episcopalist" rather than "papalist" theology. When Cyprian speaks of the "chair of Peter," he does so in a symbolic sense. Christ bestowed the power on Peter first, not to make him superior to the other Apostles, but to symbolize that the desired unity/oneness is a basic value for the Church. In this sense, every legitimate bishop in the Church has the "chair of Peter." In letter 59.14 Cyprian comes closest to identifying this mystic symbol and origin of unity in the Church with the contemporary see of Rome.

While Cornelius was bishop of Rome, all went smoothly. Cyprian had the opposite experience with Stephen of Rome (+257). Here radical disagreement on the question of the rebaptism of heretics brought about a break between Carthage and Rome. Cyprian continued to express his usual views on authority in the Church. The difficulty came to an end only with the martyrdom of Cyprian in 258.

THE UNITY OF THE CHURCH

4.[14] And if anyone should consider and examine this, no long discussions will be required. For faith such a proof is simple, given the word of the Lord. For the Lord said to Peter: "I say to you that you are Peter and on this rock I shall build my Church and the gates of Hell shall not conquer it. I will give you the keys of the kingdom of heaven and what you shall bind on earth, will be bound in heaven, and whatever you loose on earth, will be loosed as well in heaven." (Mt 16.18-19) He builds the Church on one man, and although he gives a similar power to all the Apostles after the resurrection and says: "As the Father sent me, I also send you; Receive the Holy Spirit; If you remit the sins of anyone, they will be remitted; if you retain them, they will be retained." (Jn 20.21,23), still, in order that the unity be made absolutely clear, he arranged by his authority that the origin of that same unity begin from one man. To be sure, the other Apostles were what Peter was, endowed with equal honor and power, but unity takes its origin from one person in order that the Church of Christ might be shown forth as one and united. The Holy Spirit, in the Lord's name, underlines this unity of the Church when he says in the Song of Songs: "One alone is my dove, my perfect one, her mother's chosen, the dear one of her parent." (Sg 6.9) Can the one who does not maintain this unity of the Church really believe that he maintains the faith? Can he who

[14]Text: CCL 3. 251-253

stubbornly fights against the Church trust that he is within
the Church, when the blessed Apostle Paul teaches us this
same doctrine and shows forth the mystery of unity when he
says: "One body and one Spirit, one hope of your calling,
one Lord, one faith, one baptism, one God." (Eph 4.4 f.)

5. And we bishops above all, we who are leaders in the
Church, we are obliged firmly to hold and defend this unity
so that we may show forth the episcopal authority as one
and undivided. Let no one trick the brethren with a lie; let no
one corrupt the truth of the faith by faithless misrepresenta-
tion. For the authority of the episcopate is one, with each
bishop holding his part in its totality.

LETTER 59 TO CORNELIUS OF ROME

59.14[15] It was not enough for them to have departed from
the Gospel, to have deprived the fallen of the hope of
making satisfaction and doing penance. Nor was it sufficient that they took away all feeling for penance and its
fruits from those involved in swindles, tainted by adultery,
polluted by the deadly contagion of the sacrifices, out of the
fear that they might beseech God, that they might do public
penance in church for their sins. Further, they have now set
themselves up outside of, and indeed against, the Church, a
conventicle for their doomed splinter group. Here is the spot
these people with their bad consciences will gravitate
toward, the same ones who refuse to pray and make good to
God.

Now, to top it all, after setting up a pseudo-bishop for
themselves, these heretics dare to set sail for the Chair of
Peter and to that quintessential church from which radiates
outward the unity of the episcopate. They bear letters from
schismatics and unholy persons, giving no thought to the
fact that these are the Christians of Rome, the very ones
whose faith was praised by the Apostle, to whom faithlessness can have no entree. What possible reason could they

---

[15]Text: ed. Bayard, *Correspondence*, II. 183-184

have for coming to announce that a false bishop has been set up against the real bishops? Either they like what they have done and are sticking with it, or, if they now dislike it and are turning around, they know where they should turn.

For all of us together have decided, and it is altogether just and equitable that each case should be heard where the transgression was committed. Different parts of the flock have been assigned to individual shepherds. Each shepherd should lead and govern his flock; he will give an account of his stewardship to the Lord. This being so, it is not right that those whom we lead should go running about and upsetting the harmony of the bishops with shameless lies and trickery, but should have their cases heard here where their accusers are, and where the witnesses to their crimes can testify; unless, of course, to these desperate few, the authority of the African bishops may seem insufficient, they who have already come to a verdict and have in fact recently condemned their consciences caught in the snares of many crimes.

LETTER 63 TO CECIL

Against the Aquarii

63.1[16] I know well, dearly beloved brother, that most of the bishops whom God has placed at the head of the Lord's churches throughout the entire world keep the truth of the Gospel and the tradition of the Lord. They do not depart through some human, novel inspiration from what Christ the teacher himself taught and did. Certain others, however, whether by ignorance or by simplicity when they consecrate the cup of the Lord and present it to the faithful, do not do what Jesus Christ, our Lord and our God, author and teacher of this sacrifice, did and taught. I thus consider it a sacred and necessary task to write to you on this subject so that, if there is anyone still caught in this error, seeing the light of truth, he will return to the root and origin of the Lord's tradition.

[16]Text: Bayard, II. 199-200

THE REBAPTISM CONTROVERSY

Cyprian of Carthage and Cornelius of Rome enjoyed excellent relations and cooperated closely on the question of how to deal with Christians who had lapsed during the persecution of Decius. A rigoristic splinter group led by Novatian arose as one result of the persecution. The issue that occupied Cyprian's later years resulted in part from that schism. What should be done about those who were first baptized as Christians in Novatian's church? His doctrine and liturgy were no different from those of Cornelius. The Roman solution upheld by bishop Stephen insisted that Christians not baptized in the Catholic Church were not to be baptized again when they became Catholics. Hands were imposed on them as in penance and at that moment their previous baptism became fruitful for the first time.

The African practice seems to have been similar to the Roman one up until about 220. The ecclesiology of Cyprian was (by our standards) a very narrow one. "No salvation outside the Church" is one of Cyprian's best known principles. If the Holy Spirit did not confer grace beyond the borders of the Catholic Church, obviously baptisms conferred by dissidents could be neither valid nor efficacious. By a decision of an African council some years before Cyprian became a Christian, all were to be (re)baptized upon becoming Catholics. In Cyprian's view, the erroneous customary practice of the African church before 220 had been corrected by theological "reason." The Roman custom, for which apostolic origins were claimed, was therefore also in error. Late in the controversy between Cyprian and Stephen, an Eastern bishop, Firmilian of Caesarea in Cappadocia, a student of Origen, intervened on Cyprian's side, to say that his church had always (re)baptized heretics and that this practice was apostolic in origin. The terms of the dispute thus frequently contrasted "custom" and "truth." This controversy highlights the authority of tradition and custom and the difficulties posed by the clash of customs in different parts of the Church.

Letter 67 to the Christians of Leon, Astorga and Merida

In letter 67, Cyprian advised some Christians in Spain not to take back their former bishops who had lapsed during the persecution (though Stephen of Rome had expressed the wish that they do so.) In this letter, Cyprian describes how bishops are chosen. Notice how he eliminates the distinction between Apostle and bishop.

67.4[17] Hence we see that the custom of choosing a bishop in the presence of the people, in the sight of all, so that he may be seen to be worthy and suitable by public judgment and testimony, comes from divine authority. In the book of Numbers, the Lord commanded Moses in these words: "Take Aaron, your brother, and Eleazar, his son, and bring them up the mountain in the presence of the assembly and take the garment from Aaron and put it on Eleazar his son and let Aaron die there." (Nm 20.25-26) God orders that the priest be chosen in the presence of the assembly, i.e. God is instructing us that bishops are not to be ordained except with the knowledge of the people standing by , so that, with the people present, either the sins of the wicked may be uncovered or the merits of the good be made known. That ordination will be just and legitimate which has been tested by the judgment and decision of all. Later, in accord with divine teachings, this was done in the Acts of the Apostles. Concerning a bishop to be ordained in the place of Judas, Peter spoke to the people: "Peter arose in the midst of the disciples; there was a crowd gathered. . . "(Acts 1.15) We see that the Apostles followed this procedure not only in choosing bishops and priests but also in the ordination of deacons concerning which it is also written in the Acts (6.2): "And the Twelve called together the whole assembly of the disciples and said to them. . . " The whole people was diligently and carefully called together lest anyone unworthy find his way to the ministry of the altar or to the place of the bishop. That the unworthy are sometimes ordained, not according to God's will but according to human presumption and that

[17]Text: Bayard, II. 229-230

those things which do not proceed from a legitimate and just ordination displease God, God himself showed when he spoke through the prophet Hosea (8.4): "They made a king for themselves but without my authority."

5. Wherefore what has been received from divine and apostolic tradition must be preserved and held on to. Thus we and almost all the provinces maintain that for ordinations to be properly carried out, all the neighboring bishops of the same province should gather, together with the people for whom a leader is to be chosen. The bishop is to be chosen in the presence of the people, the people who best know the lives of each (candidate) and who have observed his conduct.

Letter 68 to Stephen of Rome

> In letter 68, Cyprian complains that Stephen has not done something about Marcian, bishop of Arles in southern Gaul, who took a rigoristic position similar to that of Novatian. It seems that the local Christians in Gaul are to choose a new bishop, but Rome as the center of communion and communication is to send official notice to the other churches about the identity of the new bishop. In Cyprian's ecclesiology, it was vital for him and the other African bishops to be in communion with the right bishops in Gaul as elsewhere in the Church.

68.5[18] All of us everywhere have come to a final decision on this. Nor could there be differing views among us in whom there is but one Spirit. In any event, it is obvious that the one whom we see holding different views does not hold the truth of the Holy Spirit with the others. Let us know who has been chosen in the place of Marcian of Arles so that we may know to whom we should direct our fellow bishops and to whom we ought to write.

[18]Text: Bayard, II. 238

The Council of Carthage of 1 September, 256[19]

On the first of September, many bishops from the provinces of Africa (Proconsularis), Numidia and Mauretania gathered at Carthage. There were also many presbyters and deacons together with a great part of the people. The letters of Jubaianus to Cyprian and Cyprian's answer concerning the baptism of heretics were read...

Cyprian: The Opening Address

Dear colleagues, you have heard what our fellow bishop, Jubaianus, wrote to me, consulting my humble self about the illicit and profane baptism of heretics. You have also heard my response, repeating what we have decided again and again, viz. that heretics coming to the Church must be baptized and hallowed with the Church's baptism. Another letter of Jubaianus has been read to you in which, thanks to his sincere and pious devotion, in responding to our letter, he not only agreed but also gave thanks, confessing that he had learned a lot. It remains that each of us now express openly what each one thinks about this question, judging no one, and not rejecting anyone from communion, should that person have another view. For none of us sets himself up as a bishop of bishops, or by tyrannical terror seeks to force his fellow bishops to the necessity of obeying; since each bishop has his own views in the use of his freedom and authority and so cannot be judged by another, any more than he has a right to judge another. But let us all await the judgment of our Lord Jesus Christ, who alone has the sole power both to set us in authority over his Church and to judge our actions.

Letter 71 to Quintus

71.3[20] We shall not rule things out in advance because of custom but we should overcome by reason. For neither did Peter whom the Lord chose first and on whom he built his Church, when later Paul differed with him concerning

---

[19]Text: CSEL 3. 435-436
[20]Text: Bayard, II. 258

circumcision, insolently claim anything for himself or arrogantly assume it so that he might say that he held a primacy and must be obeyed by newcomers who came after him. He did not look down on Paul because he had earlier been a persecutor of the Church, but accepted true advice and agreed without difficulty to the correct arguments which Paul proposed. He thus showed us the proof of his patience and his desire for unity. He showed further that we should not stubbornly insist on our own opinion but that when useful and salutary suggestions are made by our brothers and colleagues — provided they are true and legitimate — we should make them our own.

Paul also shared this outlook and, faithfully keeping in view both harmony and peace, wrote as follows in his letter: "Let no more than two or three prophets speak, and let the rest judge the worth of what they say. If another, sitting by, should happen to receive a revelation, the first ones should then keep quiet." (1 Cor 14.29-30) Thus he taught and showed that many things are better revealed to individuals and that each person should not battle stubbornly for something he once learned and held but if something better and more useful turns up, he should embrace it willingly. For we are not beaten when something better is offered to us but we learn, especially in those things which pertain to the unity of the Church and the truth of our hope and faith so that we, bishops of God, those whom he willed to place in charge of his Church, may know that there is no remission of sins except in the Church...

Letter 74 to Pompeius

74.9[21] Nor should a custom, which crept in among certain ones, be able to impede the victory of the truth. For a custom that has no real basis in tradition simply indicates that an error has been accepted as the truth for a long time. So, abandoning the error, let us follow the truth, knowing that in Ezra, truth also conquered, as it is written: Truth

[21]Text: Bayard, II. 285-287

endures and is strong forever, and lives and prevails forever and ever. With her there is no partiality or preference, but she does what is right...and there is nothing unrighteous in her judgment. To her belongs the strength and the kingship and the power and the majesty of all the ages. Blessed be the God of Truth. (I Esdras 4.38-40) And in his Gospel, Christ shows us this truth when he says: "I am the Truth."(Jn 14.6) Wherefore if we are in Christ and we have Christ in us and if we remain in the truth and the truth remains in us, let us hold firm to those things that are true.

10. ...The blessed Apostle Paul writes to Timothy and warns that the bishop ought not to be quarrelsome or contentious but gentle and docile. He who is meek and mild and has the patience to learn is docile. For bishops should not only teach but they should learn as well, for he who daily grows and makes progress by learning better things will be a better teacher... But there is a quick way for religion and for upright minds both to put down an error and to find the truth and to bring it forth. If we return to the source and origin of divine tradition, human error ceases and, once the overall design of the heavenly mysteries has been grasped, that which remained obscure under the clouds and mist of darkness is opened out into the light of truth... And the bishops of God ought to do this now, keeping the divine precepts so that if at any point the truth has become uncertain or (its light) has faltered, we should turn back both to its origins in the Lord and to the Gospel and apostolic tradition. In this way our current course of action will have the very same sources as our original ministry and office.

Firmilian of Caesarea Letter 75 to Cyprian
75.6[22] That those who are in Rome do not in all things observe what has been handed down from the beginning and vainly claim the authority of the Apostles, anyone can see. It is clear that concerning those days on which Easter is celebrated or concerning many other religious observances,

[22]Text: Bayard, II. 293, 301-303

there are differences among them. Similarly they do not follow precisely what is observed in Jerusalem. To be sure, in other provinces, there are many variations according to the diversity of people and places. Despite these variations, there have not been departures from the peace and unity of the Catholic Church. Yet this is just what Stephen has now dared to do. Against you he has broken the peace which his predecessors have always maintained with you and have combined with a feeling of love and mutual respect. Beyond that he dishonors the blessed Apostles Peter and Paul by claiming that it was they who left behind this tradition —those same Apostles who in their letters cursed heretics and ordered us to avoid them. Hence it appears that this tradition which supports heretics and which claims for them the baptism which belongs to the Church alone is a merely human tradition.

17. And here I am justly outraged at such open and clear stupidity in Stephen. Does he who is so proud of the rank of his episcopal see and who claims for himself the honor of being the successor of Peter on whom the foundations of the Church were established, not see that he is bringing into existence other rocks and many new churches since he, by his authority, defends the reality of their baptism? For those who are baptized doubtless fill up the ranks of the Church. But the one who approves of their baptism also by that fact confirms that a Church exists there, composed of those baptized persons. For he does not understand that by thus betraying and deserting unity, the truth of the Christian rock is being obscured by him and in some sense, de-stroyed... Stephen who claims that he, through a succes-sion, possesses the chair of Peter is not stirred by a zeal against heretics, granting them not some small power but the greatest of graces.

19. On this point, you, the Africans, can say to Stephen that after learning the truth, you have given up the error of custom. As for ourselves, we join custom to truth, and to the custom of the Romans we oppose another custom, but a true one, faithfully observing since the beginning the tradi-tion left us by Christ and the Apostles... As some among us

had doubts on the subject of the baptism given by those who while accepting the new prophets seemed nevertheless to recognize the same Father and the same Son as we, we gathered in great numbers at Iconium. Having studied the question closely, we held to our rejection of any baptism which takes place outside the Church.

Chapter Five

CONFLICTS AND TRADITION: THE CHURCH OF THE EMPIRE

I. Conflicts: Councils

The Council of Arles A.D. 314

The council of Arles was a large council of the West, called by the emperor Constantine in the hope of settling the schism that had broken out in North Africa after the persecution of Diocletian. The problem was similar to that experienced by Cyprian some sixty years before. But the later Donatist schism had much more serious and long-lasting consequences. The proceedings of the council have been lost for the most part but the letter of the council to Pope Sylvester in Rome shows the importance of Rome as the center of communion and communication.

EXCERPT FROM THE LETTER TO POPE SYLVESTER[1]

We also agreed to write first to you who hold the greater dioceses, that by you especially they (the decisions of the council) should be brought to the knowledge of all.

[1]Text: C.H. Turner, ed. *Ecclesiae occidentalis monumenta iuris antiquissima* Oxford 1913, vol. 1,2. 383-384

A CANON OF THE COUNCIL

1. In the first place concerning the observation of the Sunday of the Pasch: Let it be observed by us throughout the whole world on the same day and time. You (Pope Sylvester) should write to all about this according to custom.

The Council of Nicaea A.D. 325

Constantine I (+337) had no sooner become emperor of the East in 324 than he found serious doctrinal difficulties there as well, in this case the Trinitarian controversy known as Arianism. The council of Nicaea of 325, considered traditionally as the first in the series of ecumenical councils, was largely an Eastern council. Its sixth canon, vague as it is, gives evidence of the origins of what would later develop as the system of the Patriarchates. The most important sees of the East, the ancient centers of Alexandria and Antioch, Constantinople the newcomer, Jerusalem, the neglected point of origin, and Rome, the see of Peter and sole apostolic see of the Latin West, became the principal power centers of the Church of the Christian empire. A later, inauthentic Latin version of the canon contained the phrase: "The Roman church has always had the primacy." But the original canon simply spoke of spheres of influence or control around these sees. As Rome had authority over central Italy, so Alexandria should have similar control in Egypt.

CANON 6[2]

Let the ancient customs prevail which are found in Egypt, Libya and the Pentapolis, such that the bishop of Alexandria has authority over all of them, for this is also customary in the case of the bishop of Rome. Likewise in

[2]Text: G. Alberigo, ed. *Conciliorum oecumenicorum decreta* 8-9

Antioch and in the other ecclesiastical jurisdictions, the order of seniority is to be kept for the churches.

CONSTANTINE, THE CHRISTIAN EMPEROR

In the ancient Church, councils were frequently regarded as the ultimate solution for doctrinal and other controversies. The emperor Constantine (+337) certainly seemed to think so. Ecumenical councils developed, of course; they did not spring full-blown out of nowhere, complete with canonical definitions of their status, composition, etc. Yet the emperor (or his ecclesiastical ghost-writer) had a high view of the decisions of Nicaea. To be sure, we cannot forget that he also had a special interest in the re-establishment of order and harmony in the Church through acceptance of the council's decisions.

Letter to the Alexandrians After Nicaea (in) Socrates, Church History
I.9[3] . . . More than three hundred bishops, noteworthy for their moderation and wisdom, were unanimous in their confirmation of one and the same faith, which is in accurate conformity to the truth expressed in the laws of God . . . Let us therefore embrace that judgment which the Almighty has presented to us . . . For that which has commended itself to the judgment of three hundred bishops cannot be other than the judgment of God, seeing that the Holy Spirit dwelling in the minds of persons of such character and dignity has effectually enlightened them respecting the divine will.

One issue we do not explore here is that of Church/ State relations. The ancient world generally did not make such a dichotomy. As the emperor had been *Pontifex maximus* of the traditional Roman religion, so Constantine and his Christian successors saw it as their duty to make sure that the Church's difficulties were resolved. This normally did not mean that the emperors dictated

[3]Text: PG 67. 85

doctrinal definitions to the Church but that the emperors saw to it that the Church had the opportunity and facilities to solve its own problems. Afterwards they made the council's decisions into imperial law. Thus the emperors convoked councils and provided bishops with transportation to get there.

Eusebius of Caesarea, the Life of Constantine

IV.24[4] Hence it was not without reason that once, on the occasion of his entertaining a company of bishops, he let fall the expression, 'that he himself was also a bishop,' addressing them in my hearing in the following words: "You are bishops whose jurisdiction is within the Church. I also am a bishop ordained by God to oversee those outside the Church." And truly his measures corresponded with his words; for he watched over all his subjects with an episcopal care and exhorted them as far as he could to lead godly lives.

THE AUTHORITY OF NICAEA

Hilary of Poitiers

Hilary, bishop of Poitiers, (c.315-367) was a leader of the Western bishops who remained faithful to Athanasius and participated in the struggle against those who rejected the council of Nicaea. He was exiled in Asia Minor for about four years during which time he was able to become more familiar with the Eastern theology.

Fragment[5] from a Lost Work

We must not depart from the creed received... and we shall not depart from the faith which we have received, through the prophets, from God the Father, through Christ our Lord, thanks to the teaching of the Holy Spirit, in the Gospels as well as in the writings of the Apostles; the faith established by the tradition of the Fathers, following the succession of the Apostles until its formulation at Nicaea,

[4]Text: GCS (*Eusebius Werke*) 1.1. 128
[5]Text: CSEL 65. 95-96

L9074

drawn up against the heresy, which arose at this time, and this formulation will remain. To all this, we believe that nothing must be added nor, obviously, can anything be taken away. We want no novelties introduced. The words, inscribed on our minds from many passages in the holy Scriptures, as well as the reality of "substance," must remain unshaken. The Catholic Church has never stopped confessing and professing this doctrine in accord with the divine teaching.

Athanasius

Athanasius (c. 296-373), bishop of Alexandria from 328-373, is best known for his sometimes lonely struggle against Arianism and the various opponents and critics of the first ecumenical council, Nicaea. Both Arians and Nicenes offered scriptural proof texts to support their arguments but Athanasius points out that a tradition of interpretation of Scripture as well as a tradition of worship must be taken into account and these point to the consubstantiality of the Son with the Father.

Against the Pagans

1[6] But since you desire to have it discussed, we shall, as much as we are able, give a brief exposition of the faith of Christ; you could discover it for yourself from the divine Words, but it is also a good thing to wish to learn about it from others. Of course, the holy Scriptures, divinely inspired, are self-sufficient for the proclamation of the truth. But there are also numerous works composed for this purpose by our blessed teachers. The one who reads them will understand the interpretation of the Scriptures and will be able to gain the knowledge he desires.

There was no pre-existent definition of what an ecumenical council is. Athanasius' own appreciation and understanding of the significance and authority of the council of Nicaea grew during the fourth century. A serious complication was introduced by the multiplication of regional councils, sometimes attended by an

[6]Text: SC 18 bis. 46

impressive number of bishops, which produced new creeds and statements, frequently under imperial coercion. These councils and creeds usually did not blatantly contradict Nicaea but more often pointedly ignored it. Two of these councils, controlled by the Arian emperor Constantius II, were called for Ariminum (West) and Seleucia (East) in 359. Athanasius comments that they have no purpose but to rubber-stamp a form of Arianism.

The Defence of the Nicene Definition

27.[7] This is what we are trying to prove: This view has been transmitted from the (earlier) Fathers to the (later) Fathers. But you, a new kind of Jews and defenders of Caiaphas, what Fathers can you show to be behind your assertions? Not one of the wise and knowledgeable Fathers but only the Devil... who now persuades you to insult the ecumenical council because it did not accept your teachings but rather those handed down by "the original eyewitnesses and ministers of the Word." (Lk 1.2) For the council confessed in writing the faith which is the same as that of the Catholic Church.

On the Councils of Ariminum and Seleucia

5[8] As to the council of Nicaea, it was not an ordinary meeting but was called to reply to a pressing need and for a most worthy end... They did not write down as the heading of this document the consul, the month and the day, but concerning Easter: "the following has been decreed." Then it was decreed that all should obey. As to the faith, they did not write: "It has been decreed" but, "Here is the faith of the Catholic Church." Then immediately they confessed what they believed, thus showing that their ideas were no novelty but of apostolic origin and that what they had written was not something they had composed but was the same as the Apostles had taught.

[7]Text: H.G. Opitz, ed. *Athanasius Werke* (1935) 24
[8]Text: Opitz, 233-234

6. But, on the contrary, on what reasonable grounds do these people call councils these days?...(The only heresies around are the teachings of the same people who are calling the council.)... What is the use of (new) councils? Nicaea is enough; it was called to oppose the Arian heresy as well as others, all of which it condemned by a sound faith...

7. Since there are no good reasons on their side and since they are lacking on all sides despite their pretences, the only thing left for them is to say: We, going against those who went before us and transgressing the traditions of the Fathers, have decided that there should be a council...

II. Tradition in the East

Cyril of Jerusalem

Cyril of Jerusalem (c. 315-386) was bishop of that city from the year 348. These catechetical instructions, probably delivered early in his episcopate, are an outstanding example of the genre — a bishop preaching to the catechumens who are to be baptized at the Easter vigil, speaking to them about the Christian mysteries. He urges them to guard well what they learn, to read only the scriptural books accepted by the Church and read publicly in the liturgy, to follow the traditional understanding of Scripture as expounded in the Church's teaching and preaching and as summarized in the Creed. Note that the discipline of the secret (*disciplina arcani*) is in force and the catechumens are not to write down the Creed they learn lest non-believers find it. (See Augustine also.)

CATECHESIS IV

IV.17[9] Concerning the divine and holy Mysteries of the faith, not even the least of them should be handed on

[9]Text: PG 33. 476-477; 496, 497

without the divine Scriptures; we must not let ourselves be innocently led astray by persuasive and well-crafted arguments. As for myself, who now say this to you, do not believe me unless you have a proof of what I proclaim from the divine Scriptures. For the saving power of our faith does not come from clever arguments but from proofs from the divine Scriptures.

IV.33 (Heretics quote Scripture for their own purposes.) Learn with eagerness and learn from the Church, what the books of the Old and the New Testaments are. But do not read the apocryphal books. Since you do not know the texts accepted by all, why bother to no avail about those which are surrounded by uncertainty?

IV.35 Study only those books which are read publicly in church. The Apostles and ancient bishops, the heads of the churches, were wise men, more devout than you. They were the ones who transmitted these Scriptures to us. You who are a child of the Church — do not falsify the rules...

CATECHESIS V

V.12[10] When you learn and confess the faith, embrace and keep only that which is now passed on to you by the Church and which is supported by the whole of the Scriptures. Since not everyone can read the Scriptures, hindered as they are from knowing them either by lack of knowledge or by lack of free time, in order that their souls not perish because of ignorance, we are going to summarize the whole teaching of the faith in a few sentences.

This I want you to memorize exactly and to go over with dedication in your own homes, not writing it down, however, but carving it by memory in your heart. I want you to keep this as a viaticum during your entire life. You must accept no other than this, even if we ourselves should change and later come to contradict what we are now teaching... For the moment listen to our words, committing to memory the faith and at the proper time, you will receive the proof

[10]Text: PG 33. 520-521, 524

from the divine Scriptures for each of these articles. The formulas of the faith have not been composed following what is pleasing to me but the most important points have been gathered from the Scriptures to make up together the unified teaching of the faith. And as the mustard seed contains numerous (future) branches in a small grain, so this very expression of the faith embraces in a few words the knowledge of piety contained in the Old and New Testaments. Look then, brothers, hold firmly to the traditions you are now receiving and inscribe them on the tablet of your heart.

Epiphanius of Salamis

Bishop Epiphanius (c. 315-403), the best known patristic figure from Cyprus, is principally remembered as a heresy-hunter. Here he also stresses the importance of ecclesiastical traditions.

PANARION

61.6[11] But for all the divine words, there is no need of allegory to grasp the meaning; what is necessary is study and understanding to know the meaning of each statement. We must have recourse to tradition, for all cannot be received from the divine Scriptures. This is why the holy Apostles handed down certain things in writings but others by traditions. As St. Paul said: "Just as I handed them on to you."(1 Cor 11.2)

John Chrysostom

St. John Chrysostom (c. 347-407) was an outstanding preacher of Antioch who later became bishop of Constantinople. His moral preaching made him many enemies

[11]Text: PG 41. 1048

among the powerful in the imperial city and resulted in his exile and death. He too stresses the importance of traditions.

HOMILY ON II THESSALONIANS

IV.2[12] "Therefore, brothers, stand firm. Hold fast to the traditions you received from us, either by our word or by letter." (2 Thes 2.15) From this comment it is clear that they did not hand on everything in the letter but there were many things left unwritten. In like manner, these things are equally worthy of belief. So also, let us consider the tradition of the Church worthy of belief. It is tradition — no one need seek further.

ON THE PRIESTHOOD

John, though a bishop and pastor, had at first aspired to a monastic vocation. His early work *On the Priesthood* was supposedly written to explain the point of view of the monk who seeks to avoid ordination. The monk has the leisure to concern himself with his own salvation and his own spiritual progress. The pastor, on the other hand, must be primarily concerned with the spiritual welfare of his people. Thus, in theory, the pastor should be far more advanced spiritually than the monk. Chrysostom's work is prophetic of much future writing on priestly spirituality. A loss of moral authority on the part of the clergy would inevitably result in damage to their leadership authority within the Church as institution.

II.2[13] The things I have been talking about, many of the faithful could do without difficulty — not only men but women as well. But when it comes to being at the head of the church and having the care of souls entrusted to you, let women and most men retreat in the face of the magnitude of the task... There should be as much difference between the

[12]Text: PG 62. 488

[13]Text: SC 272. 104-106, 118, 166, 330

shepherd and his sheep, indeed there should be a greater difference, than between the brute beasts and human beings endowed with reason. Much more important matters are at issue.

II.4 The one who by leading a life of asceticism improves himself also limits the usefulness to himself alone; while the benefit of the pastoral office reaches out to the whole people.

III.10 From what source do you think that such great troubles arise in the Church? They have no other source, in my opinion, than the choice of those who lead and their election. These are carried out haphazardly and with little forethought.

VI.8 When candidates for the priesthood are examined, we should...think of the one, (if there is such) who while living in the midst of the world and remaining near to it, is able to keep intact and unshaken purity, calm, holiness, steadiness, sobriety and all the virtues which monks are supposed to have... The one who has many faults can keep them to himself in the wilderness and they will be fairly harmless; but if he goes into the world, the only result will be that he will become a laughingstock and he will be exposing himself to great dangers...

Basil of Caesarea in Cappadocia

Basil (+379) was one of the Cappadocian Fathers along with his younger brother, Gregory of Nyssa, and their friend, Gregory of Nazianzus. This group played an important role in the final stages of the Arian controversy and the development of Trinitarian theology. One aspect of this theology concerned the question of the full divinity of the Holy Spirit. Was the Spirit consubstantial with the Father and the Son? In his treatise on the Holy Spirit, from which excerpts are translated here, Basil argues on the basis of liturgical tradition that the Trinitarian doxology which gives equal and coordinate honor to the Spirit is evidence that the Church has always accepted the Holy

Spirit as co-equal. He argues against a similar ontological interpretation of other forms of Trinitarian doxology which were being interpreted as rendering the Spirit subordinate to the Father and the Son.

As Tertullian did in the *Soldier's Crown*, Basil appeals to secret traditions to justify his case. Basil's argument is, in a sense, more momentous than that of Tertullian, because the former is attempting to argue from unwritten (i.e. non-scriptural, but not unscriptural) liturgical traditions to a doctrine of the divinity of the Holy Spirit. Yet the "secret" here does not always refer simply to their absence from Scripture. There is also the argument that these liturgical practices have been purposely hidden from pagans because of the "Discipline of the Secret" by which Christian mysteries were to be kept from profane eyes and ears. However understood, this argument from silence can be potentially dangerous insofar as it can become something of a grab-bag for those who wish to argue for almost anything.

ON THE HOLY SPIRIT

X.25[14] On the surface, we are the targets of their preparation for battle against us; they encourage each other to bring forward whatever each one has of experience or of power. But, in fact, the faith itself is the real object of their attack. This is the common purpose of all these adversaries, the enemies of sound doctrine: to shake and shatter the foundations of faith in Christ by shattering the apostolic tradition from top to bottom. Also, like debtors who claim to be in good faith, they demand proofs taken from written texts, rejecting as worthless the unwritten testimony of the Fathers.

We will not lessen the truth one bit nor, out of fear, will we break our pact with the truth. For if the Lord gave us as a salutary and necessary teaching the correct relationship of

[14]Text: SC 17 bis. 334

the Holy Spirit to the Father but if they have a different idea, that this is not the way it is, and that one must divide the Spirit off, separating him (from the Father) and relegating him to the rank of a ministering spirit, then is it not true that they have a higher regard for their own blasphemy than for the Master's ordinance? Let us set aside our combativeness and calmly consider together the evidence we have before us.

X.26 How do we come to be Christians? Through faith, everyone says. How were we saved? Because we have been reborn from on high, through the grace of baptism. What other way could there be? Having gained the knowledge of this salvation brought about by the Father, the Son and the Holy Spirit, are we about to let go the "form of the teaching"? It certainly would be an appropriate moment to groan in grand style if perchance we were to find ourselves now further away from salvation than at the moment we first believed, if we were to renounce now what we received then. It is as equally disastrous to die without baptism as it is to receive baptism and be short even one article of the traditional faith. As to the profession of faith which we set down at our baptism, when, leaving idolatry behind, we came to the living God, the person who does not at every moment keep it, and hold on to it during his whole life as to a solid protection, is alienating himself from God's promises by contradicting what he wrote in his own hand when he first professed the faith.

For if baptism is my life-principle and if the first of these days is the moment of rebirth, it is clear that the most precious words of all will be those expressed when I received the grace of adoption. Shall I, then, overcome by the foolish reasons of these people, betray the tradition which brought me to the light, which gave me the grace of knowing God, by which I have been made a child of God, whereas previously because of sin I was his enemy? Never!

I pray that when I die I shall go to God with this same faith. As for them, I exhort them to conserve the faith inviolate unto the day of Christ, to hold on to the Spirit without separating him from the Father and the Son, jealously guarding the teaching of our baptism both in the confession of the faith and in the doxology.

XXVII.66[15] Among the things taught and proclaimed that are kept in the Church, some come from teaching written down but other things have been collected from the apostolic tradition and transmitted secretly. All of these have equal authority in relation to piety and no one will fail to agree with them unless such a person is completely inexperienced in ecclesiastical affairs; for if anyone should attempt to remove non-written customs as being without force, that person would damage, albeit unknowingly, the Gospel on some essential points. Moreover the Gospel proclamation would be rendered an empty word. For example, to recall first things first and something in use everywhere —Where is it written that those who hope in our Lord Jesus Christ should be marked with the sign of the cross? Where in the Holy Scriptures are we taught to turn to the East when we pray? What saint left us writings concerning the words of the epiclesis, at the moment of the consecration of the Eucharistic bread and the cup of the blessing? The words of the Apostle and the Gospel are not enough for us; before and after, we add other words which are of great significance for the celebration and they come from non-written teaching. We also bless the baptismal water, the oil for anointing and, indeed, the baptized person himself. Where are our written sources here? Is it not rather by virtue of secret and hidden traditions? What writing taught the anointing with oil? Whence came the triple immersion? And everything else connected with baptism: renouncing Satan and his angels, where is that in Scripture? Do these things not come from that teaching kept secret and private which our Fathers kept in silence, exempted from curious inquisitiveness, knowing very well that by remaining silent, they were preserving the sacred character of the mysteries, for that which it is not permitted to the uninitiated to view would hardly be the thing to be spread around in written form. (Old Testament examples and precedents follow.)

[15]Text: SC 17 bis. 478-482

XXVII.66[16] In like manner, the Apostles and Fathers who from the very beginning set everything concerning the Church in order, also in silence and secrecy preserved for the mysteries their sacred nature, for what comes to the ear of the crowd is no longer a mystery. This is the reason for these unwritten traditions: to keep the knowledge of these doctrines from becoming, from lack of serious care, an object of scorn for the crowd. A teaching is one thing, proclamation, something else; one may keep silent about the former while the latter is obviously something to be done in public. The obscurity of many parts of Scripture makes the meaning of some teachings difficult to fathom — this too is a form of silence — for the profit of the reader. Because of such things, we all look to the East in prayer, but there are few who know that we are looking for our old homeland, that paradise which God planted in Eden toward the East.

We pray standing the first day of the week but not all know why. It is not only because, risen with Christ and before seeking the things that are above, on this day consecrated to the Resurrection, standing while we pray, we recall the grace given to us, but also because this day is in some way the image of the world to come. This is why it is at the beginning of days... Of necessity, then, the Church teaches her little ones to pray standing that day so that, by continually recalling the life which will not end, we do not neglect to prepare for that final journey. Every Pentecost is also a recalling of the Resurrection which we await in eternity... On this day also the laws of the Church have taught us to prefer to pray while standing, a visible way in which the Church brings us to leave the present and think of the future. Each time we kneel and get up again, we show by our gesture that we were pinned down by sin and the love of our Creator for us brought us back to heaven.

XXVII.67[17] A whole day would not be enough for me to discuss the mysteries of the Church which are not written down. Skipping the rest I will ask simply: By what writings

[16]Text: SC 17 bis. 484-486
[17]Text: SC 17 bis. 486-488

do we profess our faith in the Father and the Son and the Holy Spirit? So then, if we dig into the baptismal tradition, according to the logic of piety — since surely we should believe exactly as we were baptized — in order to set down a profession of faith in conformity with our baptism, let them also grant us, by the same logic, a doxology that agrees with our faith. But if, on the grounds that it is not in Scripture, they reject our doxology, let them produce for us the written proofs of the profession of faith, and of all the things we mentioned above.

Since there are so many things which are not written down, things of such great significance for the mystery of our religion, are they going to refuse us this single word which has come down to us from the Fathers and which we have found still abiding in the churches which have not been perverted, derived from genuine tradition, a word the arguments for which are not negligible and which makes no small contribution to the power of the mystery?

XXIX.71[18] Well then, to those who object that the phrase in the doxology "with the Spirit" is not attested and not found in Scripture, we will say this: If you insist on accepting nothing that is not in Scripture, then don't accept this. But if the majority of the rites with which we surround the sacraments while not found in Scripture are still accepted in the Church (along with many other things), then let us accept this as well. Moreover, it is apostolic, it seems to me, to hold on to non-written traditions: "I praise you because you always remember me and are holding fast to the traditions just as I handed them on to you." (1 Cor 11.2) and "Hold fast to the traditions you received from us either by our own word or by letter." (2 Thes 2.15), traditions such as the doxology we are discussing. Those who started it at the beginning, transmitted it to their successors and as it became even more widespread in time, it became rooted in the churches through long usage.

So, as in court, when there is no written evidence, we produce for you a crowd of witnesses, will we not obtain

[18]Text: SC 17 bis. 500-502

from you a positive verdict? I certainly think so... And if we clearly demonstrate for you that we have on our side a long period of time, will it not be perfectly natural to say: we are not the ones on trial here? Ancient teachings cannot but cause a certain emotion because of their venerable character, coming as they do from high antiquity. I am going to bring forward the list of defenders of this view...for we are not the ones who invented this. How could we do that? We are but of yesterday, to speak like Job, in relation to the long period of time of this custom.

For myself, if I must produce a personal witness, I hold on to this word as a sort of paternal inheritance, having received it from a man who spent a long life in the service of God, the same one who baptized me and urged me to become a cleric (i.e. Bishop Eusebius of Caesarea in Cappadocia). And when I search to see whether if among the ancient holy men there were not some who had used these words currently under discussion, I found many of them, whose antiquity rendered them worthy of credence and who, unlike people today, had a precise and exact knowledge. In order to join the terms in the doxology, some used the preposition, while others used the conjunction. But none of them ever thought that this made any difference at all, at least when it came to a pious orthodoxy.

XXIX.74[19] (In praise of St. Gregory the Wonderworker, Apostle of Pontus, student of Origen. +c.270.)

No practice, no word, no sacramental rite has been added beyond what he himself left to his church. For this reason the ancient rites now seem so plain to outsiders that they think something must have been left out. For those who succeeded Gregory in the governing of the Church allowed nothing to be added which came in after him. But among the things instituted by Gregory himself is the form of the doxology now being contested...

XXX.79[20] Here are all the reasons I should have kept still, yet charity pushed me in the other direction... Here is why

[19]Text: SC 17 bis. 512

[20]Text: SC 17 bis. 528

the crowds of enemies did not frighten me; on the contrary, for we have proclaimed with great assurance the truth, founding our hope on the aid of the Spirit. Would it not be a deeply evil thing if those who blaspheme the Spirit were so easily emboldened against the pious teaching and that we, who have such a powerful helper and defender, were afraid to preach the word which, coming from the tradition of the Fathers, has been faithfully preserved in memory down to our own time?

St. Gregory of Nazianzus

St. Gregory of Nazianzus (329-389), close friend of St. Basil and outstanding theologian, was also a defender of the full divinity of the Holy Spirit. In the fifth theological oration, from which an excerpt follows, he argues for what we would call the development of the doctrine of the Holy Spirit from relative obscurity to greater clarity.

THE FIFTH THEOLOGICAL ORATION (ORATION 31)

31.21[21] Again and again you come back at us: This is not found in Scripture! The Holy Spirit is not a stranger nor someone recently introduced. He has been known and revealed as much for men of the past as for people of today. All this has already been shown by many of those who have written about it and who have dealt with the divine Scriptures neither with indifference nor as a mere side-line. By looking beyond the letter to the inner reality, they have been judged worthy of seeing the inner beauty and have been illumined by the light of knowledge...If, because it is not written at all clearly that the Holy Spirit is God and the name is not often applied to him, as is the case with the Father first and then the Son, you find herein a reason to blaspheme and to surrender yourselves to this vain display

[21]Text: SC 250. 314-316, 326, 328-330

of impious words, we shall free you from this problem by giving you some brief explanations about things and names, especially as is customary in Scripture.

31.26 This is an instance where you will reach perfection only by continuing to expand. For example, the Old Testament proclaimed the Father openly, the Son more obscurely. The New Testament has clearly shown the Son but only suggested the divinity of the Spirit. In our day the Spirit lives among us and gives us a clear indication of himself. For it was not without danger — when the divinity of the Father was not yet confessed, to proclaim the Son openly; nor when the divinity of the Son was not yet admitted, to add on the Holy Spirit as a burden, to use a somewhat audacious term. Otherwise, weighed down, so to speak, by a nourishment that was too much for them and looking up into the sun with eyes still too weak, men risked losing even what they had. On the contrary, by gradual steps, and as David said, by "going from strength to strength" (Ps 84.6), by moving "from glory to glory" (2 Cor 3.18), the light of the Trinity will shine out with greater brilliance.

31.27 You see flashes of light which have gradually enlightened us, and that order of theology which it is preferable for us to keep, neither revealing things too suddenly nor keeping them hidden till the end. The first is amateurish; the second, godless. The first might shock those who are not used to it; the latter might alienate our own people. This is an idea that may have already occurred to others, but it seems to me to be the fruit of my own thinking and I am going to add it to what I have been saying. The Savior filled his disciples with a multitude of teachings but there were some things, as he himself put it, which they could not bear at that time. . .and for this reason they were kept secret. He added that the Spirit would teach us all things when he would come. I believe that one of these teachings is the divinity of the Spirit himself, made clear at a later time, at a moment when such knowledge would be opportune and capable of being grasped. The opportune time came after the Lord's glorification was accepted and the divinity of the Spirit would not be rejected simply because of its marvelous character. Could Jesus himself have promised or the Holy Spirit have taught anything more marvelous?

Theodoret of Cyrus

Theodoret, Bishop of Cyrus, (c.393-c.466) outstanding theologian and historian of the school of Antioch, had many difficulties during the time of the councils of Ephesus (431) and Chalcedon (451) because of the opposition to him from the theologians of the Alexandrian tradition. In this excerpt, he stresses the growing importance of the theological tradition taught by earlier ecclesiastical writers — the Fathers — for the understanding of Scripture in the Church.

LETTER 89 TO THE PATRICIAN FLORENS[22]

We thought it useful to call your attention to the fact that those who attack our beliefs are slandering us. We ourselves, to be sure, recognize that we have made mistakes, but we have kept untainted to this day the faith taught by the Apostles...To defend this faith, we have never stopped combatting heresies of all types. It is this faith that we never cease to feed to those who have been nourished on true piety...This teaching has been handed down to us not only by the Apostles and prophets but also by those who have interpreted their writings, Ignatius, Eustathius, Athanasius, Basil, Gregory, John and the other lights of the world and before them, by the holy Fathers gathered at Nicaea whose confession of faith we have kept intact, as the inheritance from a Father, while those who dare to violate their teachings, we call corrupt and enemies of the truth.

[22]Text: SC 98. 236, 238

Chapter Six

ANOTHER KIND OF AUTHORITY: SPIRITUAL AUTHORITY IN CONFLICT WITH THE INSTITUTION?

Those who suffered for Christ, the martyrs, were those who imitated Christ to the fullest degree. If they truly followed him to the end, they died and were the only Christians, so many believed at the time, who entered heaven immediately after death. Those who were imprisoned, tortured but survived were considered specially gifted with spiritual blessings, not only for themselves but for others. Their blessing was sought by sinners in need of forgiveness. In this first excerpt, from an important account of martyrdom, those who are soon to die are invited to settle a quarrel among the clergy. It may even be that if elected to church office, they were exempted from the necessity of ordination in the usual way. If that is the correct interpretation of this section from Hippolytus' *Apostolic Tradition*, the privilege did not survive much longer.

The Martyrdom of Perpetua and Felicity

13.[1] We went out and saw in front of the gates Optatus the bishop on the right and Aspasius the presbyter on the left.

[1]Text: H. Musurillo, ed. *The Acts of the Christian Martyrs* Oxford Early Christian Texts 120, 122

They stood apart and were downcast. They fell at our feet and said: Help bring us back together. You have gone off and left us this way. And we said to them: But are you not our Father in God and you, our presbyter? Why do you fall at our feet? We were moved and embraced them. Perpetua then began to speak to them in Greek. And we took them aside in a garden under a rose arbor. While we were talking, angels said to the clergy: "Let these people continue their journey that they may be refreshed. If you have disagreements, settle them yourselves." They were upset. The angels said to Optatus: "Admonish your people. They gather for worship as if they were coming in from the races, and quarreling over the results." It seemed to us as if they wanted to close the gates. And we started to recognize many of the brethren there, including the martyrs. All were sustained by the wonderful odor which delighted us. Then I woke up happy.

14. These were the remarkable visions of the blessed martyrs Saturus and Perpetua which they themselves recorded.

Hippolytus of Rome

THE APOSTOLIC TRADITION

9.[2] If a confessor has been in chains for the name of the Lord, hands shall not be imposed on him for the diaconate nor for the presbyterate. For he has the honor of the presbyterate through his confession. If, however, he is chosen as bishop, hands shall be imposed on him. If, however, this confessor is a person who has not been brought before the authorities nor punished in chains nor put in prison, nor

[2]Text: SC 11 bis. 64

condemned to some other punishment, but who just happened to be mocked because of the name of Our Lord...if he confessed, hands will be imposed on him for whatever office he is deemed worthy of.

Athanasius of Alexandria

If there were conflicts between those who sought the path of perfection as monks and those who toiled less spectacularly as clerics, you would not know it from Athanasius' life of St. Antony of the desert. Traditionally the first hermit, Antony's life became very influential in the spread of the monastic ideal, especially in the West, and its literary form served as a pattern for similar accounts of later holy men.

THE LIFE OF ANTONY

4.[3] Antony is the "friend of God."

67. Great man though he was, Antony honored the clergy of the Church exceedingly and wanted every cleric to precede him in honor. He was not ashamed to bow his head to bishops and priests. If a deacon happened to come to him seeking help, they talked about what was helpful but in matters of prayer, he would yield to the deacon, not being ashamed to learn...

68. In questions concerning the faith, his loyalty was admirable. For example, he would never have anything to do with the Meletian schismatics, since he knew of their evil and their apostasy. Nor did he have anything to do with the Manichaeans or any other heretics, except that he exhorted them to return to the true faith. Likewise he hated the heresy of the Arians; he urged everyone to stay away from them and not to share their perverted faith...

[3]Text: PG 26. 845, 937, 940

Jerome

St. Jerome (+420) was ordained a priest in Antioch but apparently rarely exercised the ministry. He considered himself a monk. His comments here highlight the common view of the difference between the two vocations. Heliodorus who thought of becoming a monk ended as bishop of Altinum in Northern Italy.

LETTER 14 TO HELIODORUS

14.8[4] (Jerome urges upon him the necessity of leaving one's native area.) ... You will appeal to the clergy: "Shall I dare say anything about those who obviously remain in their own cities?" Far be it from me to say anything bad about the men who, succeeding to the apostolic rank, by repeating the sacred words bring down the body of Christ, by whose ministry we have become Christians, who, possessing the keys of the kingdom of heaven in some way judge us before the judgment day, and who preserve in sober chastity the Lord's bride. But as I have been trying to make you understand, the monk's calling is different from that of the clergy. The clergy feed the sheep; I am among those who are fed...

14.9 Not all the bishops are real bishops. You study Peter, but take time to think of Judas also. You take up Stephen but have a look at Nicholas as well, the one whom the Lord in the Apocalypse said he hated...Let each one take a good look at himself before he steps forward. Ecclesiastical position does not make a man a Christian...Jesus loves the least of his disciples the most...If a monk falls, the priest will pray for him, but who will intercede when the priest falls?

[4]Text: CSEL 54. 55, 57-58

LETTER 52 TO NEPOTIAN
(NEPHEW OF HELIODORUS)

52.5[5] The cleric is the servant of Christ's Church...Let your table welcome the poor and the traveller and with them Christ will be your guest. Flee like the plague the cleric who is a man of business; one who has risen from poverty to riches, from a low estate to a high rank in society...You scorn gold, he loves it; you trample on wealth, he chases after it...

52.7 What a priest of Christ says should not contradict what he is thinking...Bishops too shall keep in mind that they are priests, not lords...

52.10 When they build churches these days, they put up walls, but remove the pillars; marble shines, ceiling panels glow with gold, the altars sparkle with gems but no one takes any care about the selection of Christ's ministers.

Sulpicius Severus

One phenomenon of the ancient Church that seems very odd to us was the coerced ordination. Martin of Tours (+397) was another of the great men of the patristic age who wished to be a monk but who was forced, literally by popular demand, to be a pastor. This life of Martin, one of the most popular works of the Western Middle Ages, shows the contrast and latent hostility between the non-monastic clergy, whose bishops were frequently taken from the Roman aristocracy, and the new clergy drawn from the ranks of the monks and ascetics. The spiritual man is not to fight the institution, but increasingly is brought in to lead it.

[5]Text: CSEL 54. 421-422, 427, 431

THE LIFE OF MARTIN OF TOURS

6.[6] Meanwhile the Arian heresy was spreading throughout the whole world and especially in Illyricum, while, almost alone, he (Martin) was fighting strenuously against the faithlessness of the bishops. He had numerous punishments inflicted on him. He was publicly beaten and then forced to leave the city. Coming back to Italy, and finding the Church in Gaul disturbed by the departure of Saint Hilary (of Poitiers) when the violence of the heretics had forced him into exile, he decided to stay near Milan for the time being.

9. About this same time, he was sought for the episcopate of the church of the city of Tours. But since it was not easy to lure him out of the monastery, a certain Rusticius, a citizen of Tours, claiming that his wife was sick, went down on his knees to get him to come out. So, with crowds of people standing along the route, he was brought to the city as if under guard. In the city, an almost unbelievable multitude of people not only from Tours but from other cities had gathered for the election. There was but one will in all, one opinion and intention: Martin was most worthy of the episcopate. The church which got such a bishop would be fortunate indeed.

A few however, including some of the bishops who had been called to ordain the bishop, impiously resisted, saying that this person was contemptible, unworthy of the episcopate, with his sorry appearance, soiled clothes, and hair in disorder. The foolishness of these men who while they tried to insult him, in fact were making him better known, was derided by the people who were of a sounder mind. In fact, they could only yield before the wishes of the people inspired by the will of the Lord. For among the bishops who were there, the leader of the opposition was a man by the name of Defensor. It was widely noticed when he was rebuked by a line in the reading taken from the prophets.

9. By chance the reader whose turn it was to read that day

---

[6]Text: SC 133. 264-266, 270-274, 294-296, 314

could not get through the crowd. Since the concern of the ministers who were looking around for the missing reader was evident, one of the bystanders took the book and started in on the first verse that caught his eye. This was the line from the psalm (Ps 8.3) "Out of the mouths of babes and sucklings, you have fashioned praise because of your foes, to silence the hostile and the vengeful." (Note: In the Latin text read then: "to silence the defender" = Defensor.) When this was read, a shout went up from the crowd and the opponents were thrown into confusion. The general view was that the psalm had been read by divine direction so that Defensor would hear this testimony against his actions. He who had helped bring to perfection in Martin the praise of the Lord out of the mouths of babes and sucklings had now been exposed and destroyed.

10. And now, what Martin's way of life after his ordination as a bishop was like, its greatness, is beyond our power to tell. With a perfect fidelity, he remained what he had been before. The same humility in his heart, the same poverty of clothing and still full of authority and grace, he fulfilled the office of a bishop without, however, abandoning either the life or the virtues of a monk.

20. I wish to mention some minor incidents among so many great matters — although because our times are such that all things seem corrupt and depraved, it is no minor event when a bishop's principles do not sink to flattering a ruler. Many bishops from various regions came together to meet the emperor (Magnus) Maximus, a man of fierce pride, puffed up by his victory in the civil war. Their disgusting fawning upon the emperor was taken note of and because of such weakness, the dignity of bishops was cravenly reduced to that of royal courtiers. In Martin alone, apostolic authority remained undiminished. For even when it was the case that he had to petition the prince on behalf of several people, he demanded rather than begged and despite the repeated invitations of the ruler, he refrained from dining with him, saying that he could not share a meal with someone who had deprived one emperor of his sovereignty and another of his life.

27. Often he used to weep for the sins of those who apparently were his detractors, who tore at him, distant and silent though he was, with poisoned tongue and serpentine fangs. Truly we personally knew some who envied his virtuous life, who hated in him what they did not see in themselves and what they were unable to imitate. Terrible and lamentable as it is to say it — nevertheless, it has to be said that though his tormentors were few in number, most of them were bishops!

Ammianus Marcellinus

Ammianus Marcellinus (+ c.395) the last great pagan historian of Rome, occasionally mentioned events in the Christian Church. He was fairly even-handed in his treatment. This report gives evidence of the growing wealth and power of the Church. Even he is aware of the problems this situation posed for earlier Christian ideals and for the moral authority of the clergy.

HISTORY, 366 A.D.

XXVII.3.12[7] Damasus and Ursinus, burning with a superhuman desire to seize the bishop's office, engaged in a bitter conflict when their interests diverged. Their supporters engaged in battles which resulted in casualties and even fatalities. And since Viventius (the Prefect of the City) was not able to stop or even reduce this strife, he was forced by the violence to leave the city.

XXVII.3.13 Finally Damasus won this contest by the victory of the party which fought for him. It is well-known that in the basilica of Sicininus, where Christians gather to worship, on one day 137 bodies were found...

XXVII.3.14 Considering the ostentatious display of life in the City, I do not deny that those who want to be part of it ought to fight hard to get what they want. If and when they

[7]Text: Loeb Classical Library: Ammianus, vol. 3. 18-20

get it, they will be carefree, enriched by gifts from wealthy ladies, ride about seated in carriages, smartly dressed, putting on lavish banquets which surpass even royal social events. They might be able to be truly happy if they, putting aside the importance of the City which they use as an excuse to justify their extravagances, they would live more like some of the bishops in the provinces. Their moderation in eating and drinking, the poverty of their clothing and their humble demeanour all commend them as pure and reverent men to the eternal Godhead and to those who worship him in truth.

Chapter Seven

AUGUSTINE OF HIPPO (354-430)

Reason — Authority — Holy Scripture

St. Augustine of Hippo, the greatest of the Western Fathers, does not discuss the question of doctrinal authority in any one place. The various adversaries, the Donatists, the Manichaeans, the Pelagians, he combatted in his lifetime, all had an influence on the way he viewed authority in the Church. In his early days as a Christian convert, influenced by Neoplatonism, he valued the authority of reason. Because of the human condition, however, in matters of religion especially, he felt authority was also necessary. What authority? First of all, the Holy Scriptures. In his pre-conversion days, Augustine, like many intellectuals of the time, was put off by the barbaric external style of Scripture. It was the preaching of his future mentor, bishop Ambrose of Milan, who first showed him that if one could get past the initial barrier, Holy Scripture was revealed as a treasure-house of the truth. It was a great repository of mysteries for those able to penetrate beyond the surface. For those unable to do that, even the letter of Scripture provided superabundant spiritual nourishment for simpler souls. Scripture, then, for Augustine remained the Word of God, the supreme authority for Christians, the place where God's truth guided the human race, its reason weakened by sin.

THE TRINITY

IV.6.10[1] What are these numbers doing in Scripture? Another person, I am sure, could supply other reasons at least as good as mine or perhaps better reasons. However, no one would be so stupid or inept as to claim that they are found in Scripture to no purpose, or that there are no deeper reasons why they are there. The reasons I have given have come either from the authority of the Church handed down from our predecessors, or from the testimony of the divine Scriptures themselves, or from the very notion of numbers and proportions. No sensible person will go contrary to reason, no Christian will contradict the Scriptures, no lover of peace will go against the Church.

TRUE RELIGION

24.45[2] There are two different ways — authority and reason. Authority demands belief and prepares man for reason. Reason leads to understanding and knowledge. But reason is never entirely absent from authority, for we must consider who must be believed. And the highest authority belongs to truth when it is clearly known.

THE USEFULNESS OF BELIEVING

9.21[3] True religion cannot by any means be approached without the weighty command of authority. Things must first be believed of which a man may later achieve understanding if he conduct himself well and prove himself worthy.

[1] Text: *Bibliothèque Augustinienne*, vol. 15. 366 (=BA)
[2] Text: BA 8. 84-86
[3] Text: BA 8. 256

THE MORALS OF THE CATHOLIC CHURCH

I.25.47[4] There is nothing sounder in the Catholic Church than that authority should precede reason.

AGAINST THE ACADEMICS

III.20.43[5] This above all is clear to me: never depart from the authority of Christ. I find none stronger.

ENCHIRIDION

I.5[6] Here is the beginning and the end: We begin with faith and are perfected by the vision. This is the whole of doctrine in a nutshell. The certain and proper foundation of the Catholic faith is Christ.

CONFESSIONS

VI.5.8[7] Since we were powerless to find the truth by clear reasoning, and for this very reason, we were in need of the authority of Sacred Scripture, I had already begun to believe that, in some way, you would not have granted the Scriptures such pre-eminent authority throughout the earth unless you wished that through the Scriptures people would believe in and seek you . As to that absurdity which I used to find so offensive in Scripture, now that I began to hear more plausible interpretations, I began to advert to the depth of the mysteries. For that reason, the authority of Scripture appeared to me all the more worthy of honor and belief because it was to be read by all and yet at the same time it kept back the dignity of its mysteries for a more profound understanding.

[4] Text: BA 1. 208
[5] Text: BA 4. 200
[6] Text: BA 9. 108
[7] Text: BA 13. 532

THE TRINITY

III.11.22[8] "We believe and so we speak." (2 Cor 4.13) For us there is the authority of the divine Scriptures from which we must not stray. Once the solid foundation of God's word is abandoned, we fall into a pit of our own making where neither bodily senses rule nor reason can shed its light.

ON THE GOSPEL OF JOHN

XXX.1[9] Let us hear the Gospel as if the Lord were present and let us not say: O how blessed those who were able to see him! Many of those who saw him also put him to death. Many of us have not seen but have believed. The most precious of the Lord's words were written down for us, preserved for us and are read to us and will be so read out to our descendants until the end of the world. The Lord is above but the Lord who is the truth is also here below. The Lord's Body in which he rose can be in only one place; his truth is spread everywhere. Let us listen to the Lord and what he will say to us, let us speak to him in our turn.

The Canonical Scriptures

Augustine was just as aware as Tertullian and other early authors of the manifold, conflicting interpretations of Scripture. First came problems of precisely which books comprised canonical Scripture and which were apocryphal. Once that had been determined, nothing could be allowed to weaken the authority of Scripture. When an apparently insoluble difficulty arose, any explanation other than the existence of error in the Bible was acceptable. When Jerome suggested that the confrontation between Peter and Paul in Gal 2.11 was basically play-acting rather than a genuine dispute, Augustine was

[8]Text: BA 15. 320
[9]Text: BA 72. 614-616

upset and complained that Jerome's theory was a threat
to the authority of the Scriptures. (See *Letter* 28.3)

AGAINST FAUSTUS

XI.5[10] ... The superiority of canonical authority of Old
and New Testaments has been distinguished from subse-
quent writings. This superiority, confirmed by the Apostles,
by the succession of bishops and the spread of the Church,
has been set on a lofty height and to it every faithful and
loyal mind submits... In that very superiority of canonical
sacred writings, it is not lawful to doubt the truth of whatever the canon confirms was said by even just one prophet,
Apostle or evangelist. Otherwise, there would not be one
page left by which the weakness of human ignorance is
guided, if the most salutary authority of these books is either
done away with by being scorned or thrown into uncertainty
by appearing to be threatened.

LETTER 28 TO JEROME

28.3[11] It seems to me to be most dangerous that anything
in the sacred books be considered a lie... Once even just one
white lie has been acknowledged in that supreme authority,
not one little part of those books will be left which will not
be fair game, whenever anyone may take it into his head that
something is morally difficult to do or intellectually difficult
to believe, he will invoke this most pernicious "rule,"
appealing to the excuse that the author is lying.

LETTER 82 TO JEROME

82.3[12] I confess to your charity, I have learned to offer
such great respect and honor only to the books of canonical

[10]Text: CSEL 25. 320-321
[11]Text: CSEL 34. 107-108
[12]Text: CSEL 34. 354

Scripture so that I believe most firmly that no scriptural author erred in anything. If I should find anything in Scripture which seems contrary to the truth, then I do not doubt that either the text is mistaken or the translator misunderstood what was being said or simply that I have not understood.

LETTER 148 TO FORTUNATIANUS

148.15[13] Nor are we under any obligation to regard the arguments of any person, however Catholic and praiseworthy, in the same way as the canonical Scriptures. Saving the honor due to them as human beings, we may reject or repudiate anything, if there be such, in their writings wherein they may have differed from the truth as understood with God's help by ourselves or anyone else. I wish others to have the same attitude toward my writings as I do toward the writings of others.

CHRISTIAN DOCTRINE

II.8.12[14] Here is the rule he will follow in dealing with the canonical Scriptures. Those books accepted by all of the Catholic Church will be given preference over those which certain churches do not accept. Next, concerning those books not accepted by all, preference will be given to those books accepted by the more numerous and more important churches ahead of those admitted by the less numerous and those of lesser authority. Finally, if he should find some books accepted by the more numerous churches and others by the more important churches, although this is a tough one, I think that equal authority should be given them.

[13]Text: CSEL 44. 344-345
[14]Text: BA 11. 252

The Rule of Faith and The Creed

The teaching of Scripture is contained in summary form in the Rule of Faith. By Augustine's time, this rule had become codified in the form of creeds as we know them.

SERMON 7

7.3[15] For when we are searching the Scriptures and think something which the author did not believe, we should not so think because it contradicts the rule of faith, the rule of truth, the rule of piety.

FAITH AND THE CREED

1.1[16] The Catholic faith is made known to the faithful by means of the Creed, entrusted to their memory in a text as brief as it reasonably can be. Thus beginners, those reborn in Christ, nurselings, those not yet strengthened by a diligent and spiritual study of the divine Scriptures, are given in a few words what is to be believed. Later, as they progress, all this can be explained at greater length while they grow in strength of humility and charity.

SERMON TO THE CATECHUMENS ON THE CREED

1.1[17] Receive, my sons, the Rule of Faith called the Creed. And when you receive it, write it on your heart...No one writes down the Creed that it may be read. But let your memory be your book so that you can re-read it, lest perchance forgetfulness wipe away what your diligence has acquired. What you are going to hear, this you are to believe. And what you believe, you are to be able to repeat. For the Apostle says: "Faith in the heart leads to justifica-

[15]Text: CCL 41. 71-72
[16]Text: BA 9. 18
[17]Text: PL 40. 627

tion; confession on the lips to salvation." (Rom 10.10) This is the Creed you are to repeat in your mind and give back. These words which you hear are scattered throughout the divine Scriptures; but they have been gathered and assembled together so that human beings, so weak in memory, may not have to work too hard; — so that each one can express and can hold on to what he believes. Have you come only to hear that God is almighty? No. You are going to have him as a Father, when you are born through our mother the Church.

Scripture and the Church

There is a certain reciprocity of authority between Scripture and the Church. In his polemic against the Manichaeans, Augustine rejected the Manichaean Scriptures. Why should he believe them as opposed to the Christian Scriptures? As a Catholic Christian, he finds the Church a social and religious reality, a reality that spans the world, that in its concrete examples of holiness urges him to accept the Christian Scriptures. It was in this context that Augustine wrote one of his most quoted lines: "I would not believe the Gospel unless the authority of the Catholic Church moved me to." (*Contra ep.fund.* V.6) The point is not that the authority of the Church is superior to that of Scripture. Rather, when confronted with conflicting sacred writings, it is the monumental fact of the existence of the Catholic Church and the reality of its life that supports the claim of the Bible to be the truth. The Manichaeans can make no such claim. Then in turn the Scriptures point precisely to the Catholic Church in the world as the fulfillment of the biblical prophecies about the universality of God's kingdom.

This testimony of the universal Church at any given moment, the belief and practice of the contemporary Church is a more significant authority factor for Augustine than it is for many of the Fathers. His emphasis on contemporary consensus and the witness of the universal

Church is probably due in large part to his polemic against the Donatists. One of Augustine's primary arguments against them was the patent absurdity of their position that they in Africa were the sole surviving remnant of the true Church. Their rejection of the universal Church in other lands as apostate was continually ridiculed by Augustine. Thus Augustine's insistence on the authority of what the universal Church believed and did. By the very fact that Catholic Christians so believed and acted, these beliefs and practices had authority.

LETTER 164 TO EVODIUS OF UZALIS

164.6[18] Wherever this tradition comes from, we must believe that the Church has not believed it in vain, even though the express authority of the canonical Scriptures is not brought forward for it.

AGAINST CRESCONIUS

I.33.39[19] To be sure, although on this matter, we cannot quote a clear example taken from the canonical Scriptures, at any rate, on this question, we are following the true thought of the Scriptures when we observe what has appeared good to the universal Church which the authority of these same Scriptures recommends to you; thus, since Holy Scripture cannot be mistaken, anyone fearing to be misled by the obscurity of this question has only to consult on this same subject this very Church which the Holy Scriptures point out without ambiguity. Do you hesitate to believe that the Church which is spread throughout the great masses of the people in all nations has Scripture to recommend it...?

[18]Text: CSEL 44. 526
[19]Text: BA 31. 146

AGAINST THE (MANICHAEAN) LETTER CALLED "FUNDAMENTAL"

V.6[20] But if you come across a person who does not yet believe the Gospel, what would you do, if he said to you: "I do not believe."? As for myself, I would not believe the Gospel unless the authority of the Catholic Church moved me to. If, then, I have obeyed those who said to me: "Believe the Gospel," why should I not also heed them when they tell me: "Don't believe the Manichaeans."?

SERMON 117

117.6[21] It is obvious; the faith allows it; the Catholic Church approves; it is true.

ON THE GOSPEL OF JOHN

97.4[22] "Avoid profane novelties of words." (2 Tm 2.16) He does not say simply "novelties of words" but added "profane." For there are in fact novelties of words which fit right in with the teachings of religion such as the name "Christian" itself when it began to be used... Against the impious Arian heretics, they fashioned the new expression: "Consubstantial with the Father," but nothing new was signified by such a phrase. "Homoousios" means simply: "I and the Father are one" i.e. of one substance. For if everything new is by that very fact profane, then how could the Lord have said: "I give you a new commandment" nor could the Testament be called "new" nor could a "new song" be sung throughout the whole earth.

THE TRINITY

III. Preface. 2[23] Let him (the reader) not love me more

[20]Text: BA 17. 400
[21]Text: PL 38. 665
[22]Text: CCL 36. 575
[23]Text: BA 15. 272

than the Catholic faith. May I not love myself more than Catholic truth. And so I say to the reader: do not be bound to my writings as though they were some kind of canonical Scriptures. If you should find anything in the Scriptures which you do not believe, you should believe it without hesitation; but if you find something in my writings of which you are not certain, do not hold on to it firmly until you come to understand it clearly. And so I say to you: Don't correct my writings on the basis of your own views but from the divine Scriptures or unshakable reasoning.

AGAINST THE LETTER CALLED "FUNDAMENTAL"

XIV.18[24] If therefore, I am going to believe things I do not know about, why should I not believe those things which are accepted by the common consent of learned and unlearned alike and are established by most weighty authority of all peoples?

AGAINST JULIAN (OF ECLANUM)

I.7.34[25] Will you, then, so love your error, into which you have fallen through adolescent overconfidence and human weakness, that you will separate yourself from these leaders of Catholic unity and truth, from so many different parts of the world who are in agreement among themselves on so important a question, one in which the essence of the Christian religion is involved...?

The Consensus of the Past

Beyond the consensus of the contemporary Church, Augustine, more in line with the other Fathers, stresses the consensus of antiquity. That which the Church has always believed is thereby true. The consensus of the

[24]Text: BA 17. 428
[25]Text: PL 44. 665

Fathers is important but no individual Father, least of all Augustine himself, should be considered infallible. It is the *Catholica*, the Church Catholic in time and space, that carries on the apostolic faith.

AGAINST FAUSTUS

XIII.5[26] The authority of our Scriptures, strengthened by the consent of so many nations, and confirmed by the succession of the Apostles, bishops and councils, is against you.

THE UNFINISHED WORK AGAINST JULIAN (OF ECLANUM)

I.117[27] What they learned in the Church, they (the Fathers) taught the Church.

AGAINST JULIAN

II.10.37[28] (Consensus of the Fathers) You see them gathered from various periods and regions from the East and West, not at one place to which men are forced to travel, but in one book which can travel to men.

SERMON 37

37.3[29] ...But the Church will be found to be more precious than any stones. There is no comparison. But there are also precious stones within the Church.So precious are these stones that they are called "living." There are precious stones adorning it, but the Church is itself more precious ...There are precious stones in the Church and there always have been the learned, abounding in knowledge,

[26]Text: CSEL 25. 382
[27]Text: CSEL 85,1. 134
[28]Text: PL 44. 700
[29]Text: CCL 41. 449

eloquence and instruction in the law. (Cyprian was a precious stone; so was Donatus until he strayed.)

AGAINST THE LETTER CALLED "FUNDAMENTAL"

IV.5[30] (What has made and keeps Augustine a Catholic?) The consensus of peoples and nations holds me; that authority, begun with miracles, nourished by hope, increased by charity, confirmed by antiquity, holds me; the succession of bishops, from the very chair of the Apostle Peter, to whom the Lord after his resurrection commended the feeding of his sheep, up to the present episcopate, holds me; the very name of Catholic holds me, that name that not without reason among so many heresies, this Church alone has obtained so that, while all heretics wish to be called Catholics, in fact, to any stranger asking someone where the Catholic church is, no heretic would dare direct him to his own meeting house. These are numerous and well-beloved claims of the Christian name which rightly hold the believer in the Catholic Church even when, because of the slowness of our brains or merit of our lives, the truth has not yet been shown in its totality.

The Authority of Councils

One of the most debated passages in Augustine's works is found in the second book of the Treatise on Baptism. Here, arguing against the Donatists who put excessive emphasis on the authority of Cyprian and earlier African councils, Augustine stresses the superiority of Sacred Scripture over all later writings. Cyprian, however saintly and eminent, made mistakes. Consensus is important and for Augustine the ultimate court of decision is the general council. In this passage, he seems to suggest that even general councils can be corrected, although the signifi-

[30]Text: BA 17. 396-398

cance of the verb "emendari" here implies "improve" more than the correction of earlier outright errors.

ON BAPTISM

II.3.4[31] Now, if they dare, let the proud and swollen necks of the heretics be raised against the holy humility of these words (i.e. Cyprian's opening statement in the council of Carthage of 256). You mad Donatists whom we wish to bring back to the peace and unity of holy Church and to be cured in it, what do you say to these things? You are always throwing in our faces Cyprian's letters, Cyprian's views, Cyprian's council. How do you schismatics presume to claim as your own the authority of Cyprian while you repudiate his example in favor of the peace of the Church? Who is ignorant that the canonical Scriptures both of the Old and the New Testaments are contained within clearly defined limits and that they are to be set ahead of all later letters of bishops in such a way that none can doubt or discuss whether something in Scripture is true or right?

The writings of bishops which have been written or are being written after the closing of the scriptural canon, can be censured by the wiser words of someone more expert in the area, or through the weightier authority or the more learned wisdom of other bishops or by councils, if there is something in these writings that deviates from the truth. And councils themselves, which are held in various regions and provinces without evasion yield to the authority of plenary councils which are held out of the whole Christian world and that among the plenary councils, earlier ones are often corrected (improved?) by later councils, when through greater experience, what was closed is opened and what was hidden becomes known, without any of the pomposity of sacrilegious pride or heads swollen with arrogance, or the malicious contentiousness of envy but with holy humility, in Catholic peace and Christian charity?

[31]Text: BA 29. 132-134

V.17.23[32] With these words, there are many considerations by which in this man (Cyprian) who loved the beauty of the house of the Lord and the place inhabited by his tabernacle, the brightness of his Christian charity shines forth; first because he did not hide what he thought but he expressed himself in a kindly and peaceable way so that he never broke with those with whom he disagreed. He understood how great are the benefits of the bond of unity which he loved so much and zealously guarded because he knew well that even those who think differently can remain in the bond of charity. It was not a question of keeping divine concord and the Lord's peace with the wicked...

...How Cyprian rejoices as he observes with greater serenity now in that light how profitable it is for the human race that something reprehensible is found in the wholesome works of Christian rhetoricians, but not in the writings of fishermen! I myself most happily join in the rejoicing of that holy soul, altogether confident that in no way are my own writings free of error...(Those baptized in heresy)...are now received according to the reasonable custom confirmed by a plenary council of the whole Christian world. I do not prefer my own opinions to that of the holy Catholic Church which Cyprian so loved and still loves, in which he bore such rich fruit with tolerance. He was not himself its universality but he remained in its universality, this Catholic root he never deserted but in this root he was fruitful; so that he might be even more fruitful, he was pruned by the heavenly vine-tender. On behalf of its peace and salvation, he did not wish the grain to be uprooted with the weeds. He both blamed the sins of men united with him by speaking the truth openly and supported them by virtue of his charity.

[32]Text: BA 29. 362-368

Chapter Eight

VINCENT OF LERINS: THE CLASSIC EXPRESSION OF THE SYNTHESIS

Vincent, a monk of the monastery of Lerins, an island off the coast of southern Gaul near Cannes, wrote his work, *Commonitoria*, three years after the council of Ephesus, in 434. It is a classic summing up of the ancient Western view. Scripture is the supreme authority but problems begin immediately when one begins to interpret the Bible. It has frequently been maintained that Vincent as a monk was writing against some of the ideas of the aged Augustine concerning predestination, ideas which posed great difficulties for ascetics. Whatever the truth of that may be, Vincent strongly warned against the danger of blindly following one man, however great and brilliant. He clearly comes down on the side of consensus, in favor of a universal council, when such existed, for the settling of a particular issue. If there is no relevant council, one must discern the consensus of the past and present. Hence the so-called Vincentian canon — universality, antiquity, consent. Moderns are skeptical about the possibility of finding such a genuine consensus among the Fathers. The treatise fostered the backward-looking view of Church History which has prevailed since patristic times.

THE COMMONITORIES

I.2[1] Often, therefore, with great eagerness and concentration I sought from as many as possible, men of outstanding holiness and learning, how I might be able to distinguish with certainty and by some general rule-of-thumb the truth of the Catholic faith from the lies of heretical depravity. In almost every case, I came away with a solution such as the following: whenever I, or anyone else, wanted to detect the lies of heretics, to avoid traps, and to preserve the faith sound and whole, it would be necessary, with the Lord's help, to fortify one's faith in a two-fold way: first, by the authority of the divine law, and second, by the tradition of the Catholic Church.

Perhaps someone may ask: Since the canon of Scripture is closed and is in all points more than sufficient, why is it necessary to add to it the authority of the Church's interpretation? The reason is this: Because of its profundity, all do not understand Scripture in one and the same way. But some interpret it one way and others, another way almost to the point that you can come up with nearly as many interpretations as there are readers and hearers. Just see how Novatian says one thing, Sabellius another, and Donatus a third, not to mention Arius, Eunomius, and Macedonius. Beyond even these there are different explanations by Photinus, Apollinarius, Priscillian. Still more: Jovinian, Pelagius, Celestius and last, but not least, Nestorius. Clearly then, lest we be caught in the twisting tentacles of ever-changing error, it is absolutely necessary that both the Old and New Testaments be read and understood in accordance with the tradition of the Catholic Church.

Within the Catholic Church itself, great care must be

[1]Text: R.S. Moxon, ed. *The Commonitorium of Vincentius of Lerins* Cambridge 1915, 7-13

taken that we hold on to that which has been believed everywhere, at all times, by all the faithful. This is what is truly and properly '*Catholic*' as the very force and meaning of the name 'catholic' indicates i.e. it includes everything universally . This will be the case if we follow universality, antiquity, consent. We shall follow universality in this way — if we confess that to be the one true faith which is confessed by the whole Church throughout the world; Antiquity, if we never depart from the meaning which our forefathers declared sacrosanct; finally , Consent, if in its very age, we hold to the decisions and convictions of all or almost all the bishops and teachers.

I.3 In view of this, what should the Catholic Christian do if some part of the Church should break off from the communion of the universal faith? What, indeed, except that he put the health of the whole body ahead of the diseased and dying member? What if some new contagion threatens to infect not just a small part but the entire Church? In this case, he will take care to cling to antiquity which cannot be seduced by any fraudulent novelty. What if an error is detected in antiquity itself, on the part of two or three individuals or a city or even some province? Then he will by all means take care to give preference to the decisions of an earlier universal council (if any) over the foolish audacity of a few people. But what if something should arise and no such clear decisions can be found? Then he must get to work to gather together and consult the teachings of the past especially of those who in various times and places remained in the faith and communion of the one Catholic Church and thus are approved teachers. And here I am not talking about something taught by one or two only but what you know was held, written about, taught by all equally in one and the same assent openly, frequently and consistently — This is what is to be believed without hesitation.

I.10[2] Someone may ask: Why does it happen so often that God permits some of the outstanding people in the Church

[2]Text: Moxon, 37-39

to teach new doctrines to Catholics? This is a good question, one that deserves a long and careful response. This is an answer that does not emerge from my own musings but is found in the divine Scriptures and the Church's traditional teaching. Let us listen to Moses. He will teach us why learned men, even some called prophets by the Apostle because of their God-given knowledge, are sometimes permitted to put forward new teachings. The Old Testament according to its own allegorical way sometimes referred to them as "foreign gods" for these ideas are honored by heretics just as foreign gods by the pagans. Moses writes in Deuteronomy: "If there arise among you a prophet or a dreamer" — i.e. a teacher in the Church who, his followers or hearers believe received his teaching from some revelation, what then? "Who promises you a sign or wonder...and what he promises comes to pass." (Dt 13.1-3) Clearly he has some great teacher or other in mind, one of such great knowledge that he seems to his own followers at least to know not only human affairs but to fore-know what is beyond man, someone such as their disciples boast a Valentinus, a Donatus, a Photinus or an Apollinarius to be — and? "And he urges you to follow strange gods whom you have not known and to serve them." Who are these 'strange gods' but foreign errors? "Whom you did not know" i.e. new and unheard of things. "And let us serve them " i.e. let us believe them, let us follow them, And finally? "Pay no attention," says Moses, "to the words of that prophet or dreamer"? And why, I ask you, does God not stop people from teaching what he commands you not to listen to? Because Moses says, "The Lord your God is testing you to learn whether you really love him with all your heart and with all your soul." (Dt 13.4) So now you see clearly the reason why Divine Providence sometimes allows certain teachers in the Church to put forward some new ideas. "The Lord your God is testing you." And the great test is when someone you considered to be a prophet, a follower of prophets, a teacher of and fighter for the truth, someone whom you have embraced with great veneration and love, this very person has subtly brought in dangerous errors which you have not been able immediately to detect because you are under the spell of this man and you cannot easily bring yourself to condemn him while affection for your teacher holds you.

I.20[3] Since this is the case, the true Catholic is the one who loves God's truth, the Church, the Body of Christ. He puts nothing before God's religion, the Catholic faith, nor does he cling to the authority, the love, the brilliance, the eloquence, the philosophy of any one man, but despising all these things, firmly and unshakably fixed in his faith, he believes that the only thing to be believed and held is that which he knows the whole Catholic Church has held from ancient times. On the contrary, he is aware that any kind of new and unprecedented idea brought in contrary to the holy ones of old, has nothing to do with religion but is a test, as he has learned from the words of the holy Apostle Paul. This is just what he notes in I Cor. (11.19) "There may even have to be factions among you for the tried and true to stand out clearly." Or he might have put it this way: For this reason God does not immediately root out the authors of heresies so that you may have a chance to show yourself "tried and true": that each one may stand out a faithful and firm Catholic believer.

I.22[4] It is worth the effort to study carefully the whole of the Apostle's chapter (i.e. 1 Tm 6). "O Timothy, guard what has been committed to you. Stay clear of worldly, idle talk." (v.20) "O". This exclamation is a sign of both foreknowledge and love. He foresaw the errors to come and mourned in advance. Who fulfills the role of Timothy today but the entire Church as a whole or, more particularly, the entire body of Church leaders who have the obligation to see that the knowledge of the revealed religion is kept pure and is so passed on to others? What does "Guard what has been committed" mean? He uses the word "Guard," having in mind thieves and enemies who "while men are sleeping" sow weeds among the "good seed" which the "Son of man"

[3]Text: Moxon, 79-80
[4]Text: Moxon, 86-95

sowed "in his field." "Guard what has been committed." What has been "committed"? This means: what has been entrusted to you, not what has been found by you; what you have received, not what you have thought up; a matter not of creativity but of teaching, not for private use, but for public preaching; something brought to you, not produced by you; a matter of which you are the keeper, not the source, not the master but the disciple, not the leader but the follower. "Guard what has been committed to you." Keep the precious coin of the Catholic faith clean and unblemished. You are both to keep and to hand on that which has been committed to you. You have been given gold; be sure that it is gold you hand on. No substitution is allowed. I do not want you shamelessly to switch the gold for lead or, fraudulently, for bronze. I want the real thing, not just something that looks like it. "O Timothy," O bishop, preacher, teacher, if the divine gift has made you fit in genius, in experience, in teaching to be the Beseleel of the spiritual Temple, chisel out the precious stones of divine teaching, join them together in the proper way, adorn them with wisdom, add, as you can, brightness, charm, elegance. When you explain the Scriptures, may what was formerly believed in obscurity now be understood clearly. Through you may future generations rejoice in their understanding of what was formerly honored only for its antiquity. Just be sure that you teach the same things that you yourself learned so that, though you may say things in a novel way, you do not teach novelties.

I.23 But perhaps someone may object: Does this mean that in the Church of Christ, religion can never make any advances? No, there can be the greatest progress. Who is so envious of his fellow human beings, so hated by God that he would try to stop it? The important point to watch is this: that it is real progress of the faith, not a change in the faith. Progress means that each thing grows within itself; change, on the other hand, means that one thing is changed into something else. So, by all means, there must be growth. Let understanding, knowledge, and wisdom progress in quantity and penetration whether of individuals or of all, of one man or the whole Church, with the passing of generations and centuries — but only so long as, at the very least, they remain the same, i.e. the same teaching in the same sense and the same meaning.

Let the progress of religion in the soul follow the growth of the body. Despite the passage of the years when they develop and fill out, still they basically remain what they were. A lot goes on between the flowering of youth and the maturity of age; those who once were teenagers become old men. Yet, however much one and the same person is changed outwardly, nevertheless his nature remains what it always was and he is still the very same person. The limbs of infants at the breast are small while those of young men are large, yet they are the very same. Children have the same number of limbs as grown men and if anything develops in those of mature age, it can only be something that was already present in the seed so that there will never be anything in the elderly person that was not at least latent in the child. Hence there can be no doubt about it: This is the correct and normal process of progression according to an approved and wondrous order of growth. With the passing years all those bodily parts and only those are completed in adults which the Creator in his wisdom first put in infants. But if the human form were to be changed into some other shape or if one were to add to or subtract from the number of its members, of necessity the whole body would either die or become some kind of monster or, at the very least, be weakened.

In the same way, the teachings of the Christian religion will follow the same laws of progress, so that as the years go by, they grow stronger, are expanded with time and grow loftier with age, yet at the same time remain uncorrupt and inviolate. It is in all measures of its parts and in all its members and senses, so to speak, full and perfect. It allows no mutations, no loss of any distinctive property, no variation in outline.

For example, our forefathers sowed in the field of the Church the good wheat-seeds of the faith. It would most certainly be wicked and unseemly for us their descendants to gather the tares of spurious error in place of the genuine wheat of truth. Rather, the only right and sensible thing is that there be no discrepancy between what comes out at the end from what went in in the beginning, that from the increase of the wheat-seed of instruction that was sown, we gather the fruits of the wheat of doctrine. Thus there is no change in the properties of the original seedling even though with the passage of time, something has developed from those seeds and with tender care bears fruit. Though a certain clarity of form may have been added, still the same nature of each type remains. God forbid that those fields of roses which are the Catholic mind be turned into a jungle of thorns and thistles. God forbid that in this spiritual paradise, there come forth darnel and aconite from the branches of cinnamon and balsam. Therefore, whatever in the Church, "God's Planting," has been sown by the faith of the Fathers, this in turn must be tended and watched over by the efforts of the descendants. This should flourish and ripen in time, it should progress and be made perfect. It is perfectly right that those first teachings of the heavenly philosophy be cleansed, refined and polished in the course of time, but it is criminal if they are changed, cut down and mutilated. Let them take on a new lustre, clarity and precision but they must not lose their full and integral distinctiveness.

For if such a thing were to be allowed to this impious fraud just once, I shudder to mention how great a danger there would be of the cutting off and destruction of faith. If any part of Catholic teaching be abandoned, then there would be another, and then another. Soon at an ever accelerating pace, more and more would be thrown over as if the whole process had become customary and indeed perfectly permissible. After each part has been repudiated, one by one, what else remains but that the whole will be similarly rejected? Once novelties begin to be mixed with the ancient, foreign elements with the traditional, the profane with the sacred, of necessity it will follow that this "custom" will slip into everything. After that, nothing in the Church will be left that is uncorrupted, nothing uninfected, nothing whole, nothing pure. What had been a shrine of pure and uncorrupted truth will have become a brothel of wicked and filthy errors. But may God keep such crimes from the minds of those who are his own; let them remain the property of those driven mad with wickedness.

The Church of Christ, the unremitting and careful guardian of those teachings entrusted to it, never allows any change in them, subtracts nothing, adds nothing. It does not cut out what is necessary nor add what is unnecessary. It loses nothing of its own, steals nothing from what belongs to others, but with all its strength seeks this one objective: handling what it has received from antiquity with both faith and wisdom; if there be anything from tradition that is merely embryonic and undeveloped, it may study and polish it; whatever is clear and plain, it may strengthen and confirm; whatever is confirmed and defined, it may keep safe. In the end, what else have the decrees of the councils striven to do except this: that what before was believed in simplicity should henceforward be believed more assiduously; what was previously preached with hesitation should now be preached with greater conviction; that what was formerly honored somewhat negligently should afterwards be observed more carefully. This, I say, and nothing else, is what the Catholic Church has accomplished by the decrees of its councils when stirred to action by heretical novelties: that what it had first received from our ancestors by tradition alone, this it consigned to written documents for posterity, summarizing a great deal of material in a few words, more often, for the sake of clarifying understanding, expressing with new terms a meaning of the faith that was not new.

I.26[5] But someone may object: How can you prove that the Devil makes use of examples from the Bible? Read the Gospels where it is written: "Next the Devil took him (i.e. the Savior) and set him on the parapet of the Temple and said: If you are the Son of God, throw yourself down. It is written: 'He will bid his angels take care of you; with their hands they will support you that you may never stumble on

[5]Text: Moxon, 107-116

a stone.'" (Mt 4.5-6) What will he do to wretched men who approach the "Lord of Glory " with the words of Scripture? "If" he said "you are the Son of God, throw yourself down." Why? "It is written," he said. It is very important that we pay attention to the teaching of this passage and never forget it. If we keep in mind this Gospel teaching,when we find people coming to us with texts from the Old and New Testaments supposedly against the Catholic faith, we will not hesitate a moment to see the Devil speaking through them. For just as head once spoke to head, so now members of one body speak to the members of the other body, i.e. the members of the Body of Satan to the members of the Body of Christ, the faithless to the faithful, the sacrilegious to the religious, the heretics, in fine, to the Catholics. What do they say? "If you are the son of God, throw yourself down." This means: If you want to be a son of God and to receive the inheritance of the heavenly kingdom, "throw yourself down," i.e. down from the teaching and tradition of that lofty Church which is called the Temple of God.

When anyone asks one of these heretics who presents such arguments: Where are the proofs of your teaching that I should leave behind the world-wide and ancient faith of the Catholic Church? He will jump in before you have finished with the question: "It is written." He follows up immediately with thousands of texts and examples, from the Law, the Psalms, the Apostles, the prophets and because of these unheard of and perverse bits of exegesis, you, poor soul, will be cast headlong from the Catholic fortress into the abyss of heresy. Then they make promises which almost always succeed in misleading the careless. They dare to promise and teach that in their church, i.e. in the cozy circles of their communion, there is a special grace of God that is so totally wondrous and tailored to each individual that without any work or effort on their part, even though they neither seek nor knock, everyone in their group is so divinely destined that, borne along by angel's hands, i.e. saved by the protection of angels, they can never "dash their foot against a stone," i.e. they can never be tempted.

I.27 Now someone may object: But if the Devil and his

followers (some of whom are false apostles and others false prophets and teachers) make use of God's own words and promises, what will Catholics, the children of Mother Church, do? How will they be able to distinguish truth from falsehood in Scripture? Remember what we said at the beginning of this work must be done, what holy and learned men have handed down to us: that they interpret the divine rule according to the traditions of the universal Church and according to the rules of Catholic teaching. This means that in the Catholic and apostolic Church they must follow universality, antiquity and consent. If, at some time, a part rebel against the whole, novelty against antiquity, the dissent of one or a few dissidents against the consensus of all, or at least the great majority of Catholics, they will give preference to the integrity of the whole over the corruption of a portion; and within that universality, they put first the traditional religion over profane novelty; within that framework of antiquity, they put first the general decrees, if any, of a universal council over against the audacity of an individual or of a few; next, if nothing of the kind can be found, take the next best thing, let them follow the convergent views of the majority of the great teachers of the past. With the Lord's help, by these measures, if they are carefully and faithfully observed, the dangerous errors of rebellious heretics should be unmasked without great difficulty.

I.28 The next step, I believe, will be for me to show how the profane novelties of heretics are to be unmasked and condemned by confronting them with the concordant teachings of the old masters. I am not speaking here of bringing in the consensus of the ancient Fathers for every little question about Scripture. This consensus should be investigated by us with great diligence and followed above all in what concerns the rule of faith. But this method of attack should not be followed for every heresy but above all for new, more recent teachings only, when they first arise, while they are still prevented by lack of time from falsifying the rule of the ancient faith and are trying to spread their poisons abroad by tampering with the works of our ancestors. Otherwise heresies of long-standing that are already spread about are by no means to be attacked in this way because the passage of time has afforded them ample opportunity for pilfering from the Truth. As for these ancient abominations, be they schisms or heresies, they can be refuted only, if it must be, by the authority of the Scriptures, or, avoid them altogether, refuted and condemned as they were in ancient times by universal councils of Catholic bishops. Therefore as soon as the foul corruption of any evil error begins to break out and to put forward in its own defense some words of Sacred Scripture and to explain them in some deceitful fashion, at once you must gather together the opinions of the ancestors for interpreting Scripture. In this way, any vile novelty that is put forward will be made known for what it is and be condemned without hesitation. Of course, we mean that those opinions are to be gathered only from those Fathers who lived, taught and remained steadfast in sanctity, wisdom and fidelity in the Catholic faith and communion or who deserved to die in Christ or in their good fortune to be killed for Christ. These men are to be believed in accordance with the following provisions: This alone is to be considered certain, undoubted and definitive — whatever all or most of them in one and the same sense have clearly, frequently and consistently, (just as if they were coming to agreement in some sort of council of teachers) accepted, held, passed on, confirmed. But if someone hold something beyond or even contrary to what all have held — however saintly and learned that person may have been — whether he be a bishop, a confessor or a martyr, that idea is to be relegated strictly to his own private opinions, quite apart from any common, public, general decision. By doing this, we shall not, according to the usual sacrilegious fashion of heretics and schismatics, cast aside the ancient truth of universal teaching to follow the novel idea of one man and thus put ourselves in danger of losing our eternal salvation.

Chapter Nine

ROMAN AUTHORITY
IN LATE ANTIQUITY

Siricius

It is only from the mid-fourth century that we begin to have abundant and unambiguous evidence from the letters of the bishops of Rome. This evidence plainly shows the Roman view of itself as the supreme arbiter for the Church. In this letter, sometimes referred to as the first papal decretal, Pope Siricius (384-399) answers the questions sent to his predecessor Damasus (366-384) by a Spanish bishop. Here we cite only the opening and closing sections of the letter showing Siricius' eagerness to establish a uniform code of discipline for the Western Church. He also mentions an idea which appears with some frequency in papal writings of late antiquity, viz., that Peter lives on in each Pope and through him continues to lead the Roman church.

LETTER TO BISHOP HIMERIUS OF TARRAGONA, A.D. 385

1.1[1] The communication which you sent to our predecessor of holy memory, Damasus, found us holding his place as

[1]Text: PL 13. 1132-1133, 1146-1147

God has so ordained. When this report of yours was read in our gathering, we found as many things that were worthy of rebuke and correction as we would have liked to find worthy of praise. And since it was necessary that we succeed to the labor and cares of the one whom we succeeded by God's grace, notice being given of my elevation, we are not going to refuse an answer to your questions. For, in view of our office, we are not free to cover up nor to remain silent; upon us falls (more than on others) the duty to work harder for the Christian faith. We bear the burdens of all who are heavily laden or rather, the blessed Apostle Peter bears them in us. He, we trust, protects and watches over his heir in all the cares of this office.

I.15 We have, I believe, dear brother, clarified all the issues described in your list of difficulties. In my opinion we have given adequate answers to each problem concerning which you have asked the Roman church as the head of your body, through our son, the priest Bassianus. Now then we can only urge your brotherly zeal to even greater and more diligent observance of the canons and decretals so that these things we have now written to you, you will take steps to make known to all your fellow bishops, not just those in your own civil jurisdiction. You are to see to it that all these things that have been so carefully set out by us, together with a covering letter from yourself, are to be sent to all in Cartagena, Baetica, Lusitania, Galicia and to all those in the provinces bordering on your own. And although no bishop is permitted to be ignorant of the rules made by the Apostolic see and the venerable canonical decisions, it will be still more advantageous for you and henceforth will add to the glories of your ancient see as well, if these things, written to you in particular but meant as general regulations, be brought through your zealous efforts, to the attention of all your fellow bishops. In this way, all these salutary decisions and rulings made by us, not hastily but most carefully and prudently, may remain inviolate and all loopholes for excuses which indeed are already closed so far as we are concerned, may be shut for the future as well.

Innocent I

Pope Innocent I (402-417) further developed the Roman desire for uniformity in practice as well as in teaching. In his letter to Bishop Decentius whose see was in central Italy, Innocent buttressed this campaign by claiming that all Western churches were founded by Rome. This Roman mentality presumed that the Apostles had literally determined all details of ritual at the beginning. Rome had maintained all these without alteration. If any other church had a different liturgy, it was because it had deserted the apostolic norm. It should henceforward conform to the Roman, i.e. apostolic, model.

LETTER TO BISHOP DECENTIUS OF GUBBIO A.D. 416[2]

Who is unaware or does not observe that what was handed down to the Roman church by the Prince of the Apostles, Peter, and is still kept up to now, must be observed by all; further, that nothing is to be brought in or introduced which does not have authority or seems to have other origins? This is even more obvious when you realize that no church was ever founded in all of Italy, Gaul, Spain, Africa, Sicily or any of the islands unless the venerable Apostle Peter or his successors appointed bishops for them. See if, in any of these provinces, there is any mention of another Apostle teaching there or even being there. If they do not discover any, as indeed they cannot, then they must follow the practice of the church of Rome, from which there is no doubt they received their start . . .

[2]Text: R. Cabié, ed. *La Lettre du Pape Innocent Ier à Décentius de Gubbio* Leuven 1973, 18-20

Zosimus

Zosimus was pope for only a short time (417-418) but became embroiled in several controversies nevertheless. He appeared on one occasion to go back on his predecessor's condemnation of Pelagius. This evoked an angry letter from the African bishops. The letter cited here is Zosimus' response. At one and the same time it seeks to placate the Africans but it also re-asserts Roman authority, if anything, more strongly than before. It clearly affirms that no one in the Church can reverse or even reconsider a Roman decison.

LETTER TO BISHOP AURELIUS OF CARTHAGE AND THE AFRICAN EPISCOPATE A.D. 418

12.1[3] The tradition of the Fathers attributed so great an authority to the Apostolic see that no one would dare dispute its judgment and has preserved this for all time by canonical rules. Up to the present, through these laws, ecclesiastical discipline gives due honor to the name of Peter from whom it also derives. The ancient canons assigned this great power to the Apostle from the very promise of Christ our God so that he might loose what was bound and bind what had not been bound. A like condition of power has been given to those who have merited the inheritance of this see with his assent.

For he has, along with the care of all the churches, above all the care of this see where he sat. He permits no wavering of its privileges or its teachings because he has made its foundations firm by his name. It cannot be shaken; no one may assault it except at his own peril. Since therefore Peter is the (fountain) head of such great authority, he has confirmed the zeal of all our predecessors who came after him so that the Roman church is strengthened by all laws and discipline both human and divine.

[3]Text: PL 20. 676-677

And in this place we now hold forth. It is not hidden from you that we have now obtained the power of that same name. You do know, dearest brothers and as bishops, you have an obligation to know this: So great is our authority that no one can reconsider our decision. We have done nothing which we have not already brought to your attention in our letters. As to brothers we grant you this so that by discussing this with all — (not that we did not know what must be done, nor that we might do something which would displease you because it would be contrary to the good of the Church) — but we wanted to talk with you about a man (Pelagius) who was accused among you as you report in your letter. He came to our see to claim that he was innocent, not fleeing judgment from his original appeal. He called for his accusers to come forward; he condemned the crimes of which he had been falsely accused by rumor.

Another decision of Zosimus stirred the anger of the African bishops. This was a complex canonical dispute involving a priest named Apiarius who had been disciplined by his bishop and the issue of the right of appeal to Rome. After an initial settlement, the same problem re-asserted itself a few years later. The final letter of the African bishops strongly attacks what they considered undue Roman intervention in their internal affairs. This shows that while the influence and authority of the Roman see continued to grow and spread, it was not as an unbroken progress, even in the Latin West.

THE LETTER OF BISHOP AURELIUS OF CARTHAGE AND THE COUNCIL OF CARTHAGE TO POPE CELESTINE A.D. 424[4]

To the most beloved Lord and honored brother, Celestine... Aurelius et al...who are present in this general council of Africa at Carthage, Greetings.

[4]Text: CCL 149. 169-172

Just as your Holiness, in your letter sent through our fellow presbyter Leo, told us of your joy at welcoming Apiarius, so we would also have liked to be able to write to you about his acquittal. For your joy and ours would have seemed more certain rather than excessively premature if it had come after, rather than before, he had been given a hearing. When our holy brother and fellow bishop, Faustinus (bishop of Potenza in Italy, the Roman chief representative) arrived, we called together a council. We believed that he had been sent with him (Apiarius) so that, as through his efforts, he had previously been freed (in 419), so now the man could be acquitted through the same man's efforts of the great crimes of which he was accused at Thabraca. But the council in the course of its investigation uncovered such terrible crimes and in such numbers as to be too much even for the favoritism, (rather than impartiality) of the previously mentioned prelate. His was the work of an advocate rather than the justice of a judge. First Faustinus hindered the whole council by inflicting various insults under the pretext of asserting the privileges of the Roman church. He wanted us to restore Apiarius to communion since (he claimed) your Holiness, thinking that he had appealed (which he could not prove) had restored him to communion (which was not right); and all this you will know by reading the minutes.

After a most difficult three day investigation, during which we, with great affliction, sought out the various charges, "God, the just judge, strong and patient" cut of the delaying tactics of our brother bishop Faustinus as well as the evasions of Apiarius himself by which he sought to cover up his unspeakable vileness. For his disgusting obstinacy was curbed by which he had sought through shameless denials to hide a whole cesspool of enormities, our God compelling his conscience and making public the hidden things which he had already condemned in his heart which was like a pigsty of crimes. All of a sudden, this clever operator broke forth into a confession of all his enormities and of his own accord convicted himself of so many incredible crimes that the hope we had had by which we thought he might be cleared of such shameful things, was changed into groans. Our sadness was relieved by at least one bit of consolation — his confession, albeit unwilling, released us from the need to carry on the enquiry any longer and he himself provided some kind of remedy to his wounded conscience, Lord Brother.

With all due respect, then, we strongly urge you not to give hasty hearings to people coming to you from here nor that you show a willingness to accept into your communion those excommunicated by us. You should take note that this *was* decided by the council of Nicaea.

And if it is a good idea to be very careful in dealing with the lower clergy and the laity, then how much more did the council wish this custom to be observed when it came to bishops, lest those disciplined in their own province seem to be restored to communion by your Holiness whether over-hastily or without good reason. As befits you, let your Holiness refuse improper refuge to presbyters and other clergy. There is no decision of the Fathers which withdraws this responsibility from the African church. The decrees of Nicaea have clearly entrusted clerics of lower ranks and the bishops themselves to their metropolitans. Most wisely and justly they provided that all such problems be taken care of in the very places where they arose. They did not believe that the grace of the Holy Spirit would be lacking to any province where Christ's bishops wisely perceive and steadily hold to what is right. Above all, anyone can, if he thinks himself wronged, appeal to a council of his province or even to a general council (of Africa). Does someone perchance believe that our God can inspire a single person with justice in such cases and deny it to large numbers of bishops gathered in council? How will it be possible for such a tribunal across the Mediterranean to reach a valid verdict when the essential witnesses because of their sex or the infirmities of age or for whatever reason cannot be brought in?

We cannot find it written in any previous council of Fathers that delegates should be sent from Rome. For as to what you sent before through the same, our fellow bishop,

Faustinus, as being from the council of Nicaea...we can find no such thing in the more authentic copies...sent by Atticus, bishop of Constantinople.

Also do not send delegates, no matter who wants you to. Don't do it lest we seem to introduce the world's vain pride into Christ's Church, which offers to those who wish to see God the daylight of simplicity and humility. Now that Apiarius and all his atrocious sins have been removed from among us, we feel that we may express the hope that in view of your Holiness' justice and moderation, and saving brotherly love, Africa will never again have to put up with our brother Faustinus.

Pope Leo the Great

Leo (440-461) is usually considered the greatest of the ancient Popes. He is the first bishop of Rome from whom we have homilies as well as letters. His "Tome" was of decisive importance for the Christological definitions of the council of Chalcedon (451). Here we cite passages from two of his homilies. They stress the ongoing relationship of Peter to the contemporary bishop of Rome. They also add the important idea that when Christ bestowed authority on Peter, it was not just to demonstrate the unity of the Church (cf. Cyprian) but it was meant to illustrate as well that all authority in the Church comes to others *through* Peter. We see here the roots of later controversies about the proximate origins of episcopal authority.

SERMON 4

4.2[5] ...It is much more useful and justifiable to raise the eyes of our soul to the contemplation of the glory of the holy Apostle Peter and to celebrate this day by venerating princi-

[5]Text: CCL 138. 17-21

pally the one whom the very fount of all charisms deluged
with such abundance so that since he alone received multi-
ple gifts, nothing would pass to anyone else without his
participation... And still out of the whole world, only Peter
is chosen. He is put before the calling of all nations and at
the head of all the Apostles and all the Fathers of the
Church. Although in the people of God there are many
bishops and many pastors, Peter in his own right governs all
whom Christ rules as the head. Dearly beloved, God in his
goodness has granted to this man a great and marvelous
sharing in his power; and if he wished that other rulers have
something in common with him, he never gave anything to
others unless he gave it through him (Peter).

4.3 ... "I will give you the keys of the kingdom of
heaven..." (Mt 16.19) The right to exercise this power has
indeed passed on to the other Apostles and the institution
sprung from this decision has reached out to all the chiefs of
the Church but it was not in vain that what was announced
to all was entrusted to one. Therefore, this is entrusted to
Peter in a special way because the image of Peter is superim-
posed on every leader in the Church. Therefore the privilege
of Peter still stands everywhere so that judgment is exercised
by virtue of his right. Neither is severity too great nor
forgiveness excessive when nothing will be bound or loosed
unless blessed Peter looses or binds. As his Passion drew
near, an event that was going to shake the fidelity of his
disciples, the Lord said, "Simon, Simon, Satan has asked
for you, to sift you like wheat. But I have prayed for you,
that your faith may never fail. You in turn must strengthen
your brothers, lest you enter into temptation." (Lk 22.31-
32,46) The danger from the temptation to fear was common
to all the Apostles and all had equal need of the aid of divine
protection since the Devil wished to upset them all and
cause them to fall.

And yet the Lord shows a special care for Peter and prays
in particular for the faith of Peter, as if the future situation
would be more secure for the others if the spirit of the leader
remained unconquered. Thus in Peter the courage of all is
fortified and the aid of divine grace is so arranged that the

strength which comes to Peter through Christ, through Peter is transmitted to the Apostles.

4.4 Therefore, dearly beloved, since we see such great and divinely instituted protection bestowed on us, rightly do we rejoice in the merits and dignity of our leader, giving thanks to our eternal King and Redeemer, Jesus Christ, because he gave such great power to him when he made him ruler of the whole Church, so that if even in our own time, anything is rightly done and decided by us, it should all be attributed to the efforts and guidance of him to whom it was said: "You in turn must strengthen your brothers."

SERMON 5

5.4[6] Dearly beloved, it is not presumption on our part, when we, mindful of the divine gift, honor the day on which we were ordained. For we piously and truthfully bear witness that in everything good that we do, it is Christ who accomplishes the work of our ministry... And so we are not glorying in ourselves who can do nothing without him, but in him who makes anything at all possible. Furthermore, there is also another reason for this celebration — not only the apostolic but also the episcopal dignity of blessed Peter who has not ceased to preside over his see and continues an ongoing sharing with the eternal priest. For the solidity which he, having been made Peter the rock, received from Christ the rock, he has passed on to his heirs as well and whenever any of that firmness is shown forth, have no doubt that you are witnessing the strength of the Shepherd... (The strength of the martyrs can be seen throughout the world.)... Who can be either so ignorant of the glory of blessed Peter or so envious of it to believe that there are parts of the Church that are not governed by his concern or are not increased by his aid? In the Prince of the Apostles there is still very much alive that love of God and men which neither prison bars nor chains nor mob violence nor royal

---

[6]Text: CCL 138. 24

threats can frighten off; an unconquerable faith which, fighting, never gives up, and conquering, does not grow cold.

Pope Gelasius

Although Gelasius was Pope for only a short time (492-496), he apparently had been active and influential in Roman circles for a long time. In some ways, he is more insistent than Leo on Roman prerogatives. After the council of Chalcedon (451), some areas of the Eastern empire rejected its decisions. This caused serious political problems for the Eastern emperors, problems they sought to overcome by what the West considered unacceptable doctrinal compromises.

One of these led to the Acacian schism (482-519) between Rome and Constantinople. Gelasius expresses in his writings the ultimate in the hard-line papal position. It pitted him against the emperor. He writes of the separation of the spiritual and the temporal powers but insists that the spiritual power has the ultimate superiority.

Of all the ancient Popes, Gelasius comes closest to making explicit what later theology might term papal indefectibility. If Rome were to be allowed by God to fall into error, then who would be left to keep the rest of the Church from falling into the abyss, asked Gelasius? Finally, he expressed the Roman point of view that it alone was and in practice had to be, the sole final arbiter of the Church's doctrinal decisions. Such definitions must be in accord with Scripture, tradition, with canon law, etc. but who is to decide whether this is the case or not? A council? Gelasius maintained that Rome could accept or reject councils as it saw fit. He recalled the papal rejection of canon 28 of Chalcedon against the wishes of both council and emperor. Thus we leave antiquity with the final Roman assertion that she is the ultimate decision maker, in doctrine as well as in discipline.

LETTER 1 TO THE BISHOPS OF THE EAST

1.10[7] "But the emperor is a Catholic!" If he is in communion, we say, he is a son, not a ruler, of the Church. In what concerns religion, it is for him to learn, not to teach. He has the privileges of his power, which he has received from God to administer public affairs... But God wished that those things which concern the Church be the business of priests, not of the powers of the world. If the latter are Christian, he wanted to subject them to the Church and its priests... Almighty God wanted the lords and priests of the Christian religion to be governed by bishops and priests, not by public laws or by worldly authorities.

LETTER 12 TO THE EMPEROR ANASTASIUS

12.1[8] Glorious Son, as a native Roman, I love, honor and venerate the Roman emperor. As a Christian, I want to act according to the knowledge of the truth with one who has zeal for God. As the vicar of the apostolic see, I, insofar as I am able, will try with appropriate action to fill in what is missing wherever I find something is lacking to the fulness of the Catholic faith.

12.6[9] This is just what the apostolic see takes great care against — that because its pure roots are in the Apostle's glorious confession, that it be marred by no crack of wickedness, no contagion. For if, God forbid, something we trust could not happen, such a thing were to result, how could we dare resist any error? Whence would we seek correction for those in error? If your piety insists that the people of one city (Alexandria) cannot be brought into line, what are we to do about the entire world, if, God forbid, it were misled by us? If the entire world has been corrected after rejecting the vain traditions of their ancestors, why is the population of one city not corrected?

[7]Text: A. Thiel, ed. *Epistolae Romanorum pontificum genuinae*, t. 1. 292-293
[8]Text: Thiel, 350
[9]Text: Thiel, 353

LETTER 1 TO THE BISHOPS OF THE EAST

1.19[10] Follow the ancient faith and the things which have come down to us from the holy Fathers. Believe with us about the Incarnation of our Lord and Savior the things that they believed, and in no way depart from the teaching of the whole Church. (We are no wiser than our ancestors, nor is it right for us to interpret in some new and different way what our ancestors learned and taught. We are not more learned than they nor are we able to understand and explain the council of Nicaea in some fashion superior to the many venerable bishops who understood with wisdom and preached the faith.) Let us hold all these things together with sincere mind and true heart and there will be peace. Let us hold without spot the rules which the Church received from these same Fathers and there will be peace. Let these things be certain and unchanged among you and there will be no discord.

1.27 (If Gelasius were to concede and re-establish communion with Acacius, bishop of Constantinople, the Holy See would be tainted with the same heresy.) If we lose them (i.e. integrity of faith and communion), God forbid, how could anything ever be restored again, especially if in its summit, the apostolic see, it became attainted, something God would never allow to happen?

1.34 If I, God forbid, were to become an accomplice in the evil, then I would be in need of a remedy myself, rather than being able to offer one; and the see of blessed Peter, (something that God would never allow to happen) would be seeking a remedy from elsewhere rather than itself offering a remedy (to others).

1.39 Therefore those in the East stand firm in the Catholic faith, because they see me defending it and are encouraged by me; otherwise, if I were to give in, they will fail, or, if I should fall, God forbid, and they should still stand firm, they would rightly condemn me before God and men. They, despite persecution, have not deserted me; shall I, unpersecuted, desert them?

[10]Text: Thiel, 297-298, 302, 306, 310

LETTER 4 TO BISHOP HONORIUS OF SALONA

4.2[11] "Remove not the ancient landmark which your Fathers set up." (Prv 22.28) "Ask your Father and he will inform you; ask your elders and they will tell you." (Dt 32.7) Why do we try to go beyond the decisions of our ancestors? Why are they not good enough for us?... Are we wiser than they or will we be able to have any stability in anything at all, if we undermine what has been decided by them?

LETTER 10 TO FAUSTUS

10.9[12] It is nothing to wonder at — that they presume to blaspheme the see of the blessed Apostle Peter... And on top of this, they call us proud when the first see has never ceased offering them whatever there is of piety. They with their utter shamelessness trust they will be able to subjugate it... I will ask them this: the trial which they call for, where can it be held? With them (in the East), so that they may be the plaintiff, witnesses and judges all in one? Neither human affairs nor the integrity of the divine faith must be entrusted to such a tribunal. In matters of religion, the canons say that the ultimate judgement must come only from the apostolic see. The powers of this world? It is not for them to judge — rather they are to learn from the bishops — and above all from the vicar of blessed Peter, about divine things. No ruler of this world, however powerful, whether Christian or not, can presume to claim this for himself, unless of course, he is a persecutor.

THE BOND OF THE ANATHEMA

1.[13] They may say, as usual, that if the council of Chalcedon is allowed to stand, they will have to accept everything which apparently was done there. It must be

---

[11] Text: Thiel, 322
[12] Text: Thiel, 347
[13] Text: Thiel, 557-559

everything or, if some part can be rejected, then no part of it can stand. These people should know that only that part must be accepted by the whole Church which is in accordance with the Holy Scriptures, the tradition of our ancestors, in accordance with the canons and regulations of the Church, only that part which promotes the Catholic and Apostolic faith, communion and truth, for the accomplishment of which the apostolic see has ordered this done and has confirmed it after it had been accomplished.

But other things, those which were done or simply talked about through foolish presumption, things which the apostolic see in no way ordered, which were clearly and speedily rejected by the legates of the apostolic see, which the apostolic see, even with the emperor Marcian asking for them, in no way approved, which the bishop of Constantinople at the time, Anatolius, claimed not to have sought and did not deny was in the power of the bishop of the apostolic see; in sum, as we said, that which the apostolic see has not accepted, because it was shown to be contradictory to the privileges of the universal Church, can in no way be accepted.

Bauer, Walter, *Orthodox and ...rliest Christianity*

... Authority and Three Centuries

...he Christian Bible

...len City: Double-

...n Latin Patristic

...Authority A.D.

...(London: SCM

...ition (Theology Press, 1971).

...ruth — A Study ...d Heresy in the

Walgrave, Jan, *Unfolding Revelation* (Philadelphia: Westminster Press, 1972).

Wiles, Maurice, *The Making of Christian Doctrine — A Study in the Principles of Early Doctrinal Development* (Cambridge University Press, 1967).